Cycles and Social Choice

The True and Unabridged Story of a Most Protean Paradox

THOMAS SCHWARTZ

University of California, Los Angeles

CAMBRIDGE
UNIVERSITY PRESS

CAMBRIDGE
UNIVERSITY PRESS

University Printing House, Cambridge CB2 8BS, United Kingdom

One Liberty Plaza, 20th Floor, New York, NY 10006, USA

477 Williamstown Road, Port Melbourne, VIC 3207, Australia

314–321, 3rd Floor, Plot 3, Splendor Forum, Jasola District Centre, New Delhi – 110025, India

79 Anson Road, #06–04/06, Singapore 079906

Cambridge University Press is part of the University of Cambridge.

It furthers the University's mission by disseminating knowledge in the pursuit of education, learning, and research at the highest international levels of excellence.

www.cambridge.org
Information on this title: www.cambridge.org/9781107180918
DOI: 10.1017/9781316848371

First published 2018

Printed in the United States of America by Sheridan Books, Inc.

A catalogue record for this publication is available from the British Library.

Library of Congress Cataloging-in-Publication Data.
Names: Schwartz, Thomas, 1943– author.
Title: Cycles and social choice : the true and unabridged story of a most protean paradox / Thomas Schwartz, University of California, Los Angeles.
Description: New York, NY : Cambridge University Press, 2017.
Identifiers: LCCN 2017052586 | ISBN 9781107180918 (hardback)
Subjects: LCSH: Voting – Mathematical models. | Social choice. |
BISAC: POLITICAL SCIENCE / Government / General.
Classification: LCC JF1001 .S38 2017 | DDC 324.601–dc23
LC record available at https://lccn.loc.gov/2017052586

ISBN 978-1-107-18091-8 Hardback

To Rachel Elizabeth, Carolyn Alexandra, Oliver Thomas, and Connor James.

Contents

Acknowledgements

My creditors are too numerous for a fair accounting. But I have especially profited from knowing as well as reading the pioneering work of Peter Fishburn, Charles Plott, and Amartya Sen, soon followed by Alan Gibbard, Peter Ordeshook, Jeffrey Richelson, Norman Schofield, and five lates and greats: Mark Aizerman, Jeffrey Banks, James Buchanan, Melvin Hinich, and William Riker. Other friends and colleagues whose spoken and written words stand out in memory are John Aldrich, Edward Alemán, Fouad Aleskerov, David Austen-Smith, Taradas Bandyopadyay, Kathleen Bawn, Nuel D. Belnap, Jr., Peter Bernholz, Steven Brams, Michael Chwe, Gary Cox, Otto Davis, Darrin DeWitt, John Duggan, James Enelow, John Ferejohn, Norman Frohlich, Bernard Grofman, Thomas Hammond, Shanto Iyengar, William Keech, Roderick Kiewiet, Brian Lawson, Jeffrey Lewis, Mathew McCubbins, Nicholas Miller, Christopher Morris, Scott Moser, Michael Munger, Emerson Niou, Barry O'Neil, Joe Oppenheimer, Dennis Packard, Prasanta Pattanaik, Maggie Penn, Nicholas Rescher, Howard Rosenthal, Donald Saari, Kenneth Shepsle, Joseph Sneed, Nicolaus Tideman, Jean Tompihe, George Tsebelis, Gordon Tullock, Martin van Hees, Harrison Wagner, Michael Wallerstein, Barry Weingast, and Robert Wilson. My apologies to all those whom I have unjustly omitted.

Some of the results presented here were joint discoveries with Duggan, others with Ordeshook. As sounding boards and general sources of wisdom over the years, I wish to acknowledge debts to Duggan, McCubbins, Ordeshook, and Plott. To all this, I must add my warmest gratitude to my students Travis Baker and Raymond Alvarez for a vast amount of pivotal assistance. As always, my wife Ellie surrounded my writing efforts, this time during a winter and spring in Los Angeles and two summers in Paris, with peace and love.

Introduction

The mathematical theory of voting and social choice grew from a tiny seed of an example discovered over two centuries ago by the Marquis de Condorcet. Now called the Paradox of Voting, it shows that majority preferences can form a cycle: sometimes majorities prefer x to y, y to z, and z to x. That makes any choice from among x, y, and z unstable under majority rule: whatever may be chosen, some voters have the power to reject that choice in favor of one that they like more. Contemporary contributions to the theory still treat of cycles and instability, under majority rule and other regimes, along with all sorts of generalizations, variations, applications, implications, and interpretations. They form much of the deductive foundation of what we know and how we learn about election systems, legislative procedure, and constitutions, and to some extent private organizations, administrative processes, and exchange economies. Despite the precision of mathematics, however, or maybe because of it, the most famous contributions are more often celebrated than understood. Countless expositions and references to key findings suffer from gross error, yawing gaps, and meretricious formulation, often hidden behind needless notation.

I mean to retell the whole story of cycles and instability, their sources and consequences, as simply and soundly as possible, scrapping otiose apparatus (but without sacrificing rigor), correcting errors (though rarely naming errants), filling gaps (but sidestepping inconsequential variations and scholarly qualifications), and adding episodes never before told. Like a great flower, this story unfolds in multiple directions. Half of it is about the diverse sources of cycles. Much of that diversity comes from the cyclic relation itself: it is not always majority preference. Other relations of "social preference," of winners to losers in pairwise contests, can be cyclic too. The other half, no doubt the more interesting half to many readers, is about consequences. Cycles are not puzzles or maladies to be solved or cured but positive sources of knowledge about how and why things work when preferences, strategies, and procedures conspire to produce social or collective choices – choices attributable to all of certain actors but not to any one of them. Sometimes seen as a mark of incoherence, cycles are, in a way, the very opposite. By dint of their many and varied sources and consequences, they impart coherence to a host of diverse and apparently unconnected features of society.

In deciding what details to include and how much space to give them, I have favored hard results over blatherskite, simple results over more complicated ones to the same effect, intelligibility over impressiveness, English over needless notation, Euclidean over analytic geometry, recyclable forms of proof over single-use ones, novelty over orthodoxy, and truth over error (which I apologize for taxing your patience to correct). More important, I have favored procedure over preference. Chapter 2 is about preferential sources of cycles and instability and their absence, the ways in which different combinations of voter preferences induce or block cycles and instability. Most everything else in the first half is about procedural sources, about the sorts of procedure that allow cycles and instability and their refinements and consequences. I have emphasized procedure partly out of personal interest (I assume you prefer to read what I write about things I know most about), but partly too because a more thorough treatment of the preferential stuff would give too much space to results that look impressive, and are in technical ways, but that ultimately rest on false assumptions. More than once, and more than most authors on social-choice theory, I have invoked the admittedly unfashionable criterion of truth to separate acceptable from unacceptable assumptions, and with it sound from unsound arguments.

For readers who know something about the mathematical theory of voting and social choice, here is a selective preview. Chapter 1 begins with the Paradox of Voting itself, Condorcet's little example. There I disparage portentous interpretations and add some simple generalizations and variations, just enough to show, without any apparent mathematics, that cycles are not peculiar to majority rule or even voting – though along the way I explain the peculiar significance of majority rule and show how it can spawn much more than cycles. One of those variations is Sen's Liberal Paradox, which reveals cycles based on individual rights. It is usually illustrated with exotic or contentious examples, but I show how humdrum and ubiquitous it really is: it is exemplified by every economic exchange.

Chapter 2 addresses those preferential sources of cycles and their absence. It begins where twentieth-century research on the mathematics of voting and social choice itself began, with Duncan Black's condition of Single Peakedness, or one-dimensionality, and his famous median-stability theorem. In a world of two or more dimensions, stability gives way to near-certain instability, thanks chiefly to Charles Plott's Pairwise Symmetry theorem. That result is supposed to be mathematically challenging, but it follows almost trivially from Black's stability theorem. Alas, that and other spatial instability results have been over-interpreted: they show less than is sometimes alleged. A more revealing source of cycles and instability is issue packaging, as when votes are traded or draft laws are composed of simple measures that cannot pass separately. It is still true that a one-dimensional or single-peaked world would be free of cycles and instability, but widely cited empirical evidence of such a world, based on dimensional analysis of legislative votes, turns out to be spurious.

As a prelude to the procedural sources of cycles, I introduce Kenneth Arrow's celebrated Impossibility Theorem in Chapter 3, but only as a prelude. The theorem itself says nothing at all about cycles. It asserts a contradiction between a set of very mild background assumptions – one of them widely misinterpreted as rather restrictive – and a very strong transitivity assumption. That assumption does ban cycles, but it bans much more, and a ban on cycles alone is consistent with those background assumptions: they do not imply that cycles ever exist. I introduce Arrow anyway because Chapter 4 shows that we can add just a bit to those assumptions and get a cycle (or contradict a ban on cycles). Actually, there are several ways to do that, the first discovered by my 26-year-old self, but the one most often cited rests on a meretricious assumption, Positive Responsiveness, innocent looking but almost always false.

Another route to cycles bypasses Arrow and starts with Condorcet. Several direct generalizations of his example are on the books. Chapter 5 offers a sweeping generalization of them all, a simple sufficient condition for cycles that is demonstrably as general as possible, necessary as well as sufficient. After that I pause, in Chapter 6, to recast all those results in terms of a fixed set of feasible alternatives containing a top cycle – and one with several special properties.

Chapter 7 turns from sources to consequences, strategic ones first. One of them is strategic manipulability, the ability of voters to profit from misrepresenting their true preferences. Actually, we can generalize and assume a bit less than cycles, then use that result as a lemma to prove that manipulability is quite inescapable: any procedure for choosing among three or more alternatives must be manipulable unless it is purely dictatorial. Such is the Duggan–Schwartz Theorem. It differs from the older, widely misinterpreted Gibbard–Satterthwaite Theorem in dropping the generally false assumption of resoluteness.

Two more strategic consequences of cycles, also in Chapter 7, are about game solutions, specifically the core and the set of Nash equilibria. As framed in Chapter 6, social-choice procedures are tantamount to game forms, structures that become games when players' preferences are supplied. The core of a game is the set of outcomes that no coalition has the power and incentive to change. Its Nash equilibria are those outcomes that no single player has the power and incentive to change. A famous and obvious connection to cycles is that they make cores empty. So no social-choice procedure that allows cycles can be implemented, as we say, by the core: what the procedure produces is not, in general, the core of a game. You may be surprised to see that cycles also block implementation by the set of Nash equilibria.

Structural consequences of cycles are more numerous. Several have to do with the forms of legislative agendas, very broadly understood. In one sense, an agenda is a tree-like structure that tells us the order of pairwise votes and how later votes depend, if at all, on earlier votes. Assuming that voters act strategically, cycles make the final outcome depend on agenda structure of that sort, even when the set of alternatives on the agenda is held fixed. In another sense, the agenda is just the set of feasible outcomes. The final outcome depends on that set, of course, but how dependent it is – how sensitive to changes in that set – varies with the procedure being used. It is especially dependent when that procedure allows cycles. Yet a third kind of agenda structure consists of the combination or division of "questions," as when legislative items are assembled to form complex packages or divided into simpler components. As you have doubtless guessed, it is cycles that make the final outcome sensitive to such structural differences.

Another important structure is the division of government into constitutional components that must concur on policy and therefore can veto each other's acts. Two houses of a legislature are so related, as is the legislature as a whole, in many cases, to independent executives and courts. Offhand, that power looks like an asset, advantageous to its possessor and therefore a source of compromise and of checks and balances – but not when cycles are present. Then the veto can be downright disadvantageous, not as a thing to do but as a power to possess.

Finally, there are political parties. Often they are not imposed by law. So why are they there? And how exactly do they differ from other coalitions? The answers lie in cycles: without them, Chapter 8 concludes, there would be no parties.

Cycles are consequential in yet another way, apparently nugatory but ultimately constructive: by ruling out simple solutions to

problems of prediction and prescription, of explanation and evaluation, cycles pose questions and help produce answers that fill gaps in
knowledge. On the positive side, one of those questions is about
solutions to social-choice processes, or cooperative games: how to
predict outcomes in the face of empty cores. Another is how to explain
observed stability. On the normative side, we find the oldest question
occasioned by cycles, the one that exercised the Marquis himself and
his great mathematical contemporary and countryman, Jean Charles de
Borda: how to decide elections, or what is the ideal voting rule. Other
questions are about the measurement of utility, or preference strength,
the nature of welfare and its connection to social choice, the merits of
conventional "rationality" requirements for individual as well as social
choice, and our seemingly incurable conviction that we ought always to
make best choices from sets of alternatives that have, ineluctably, been
given us. If my explorations of those questions, in Chapters 9 and 10, do
not always end with definite answers, it is because the questions themselves are not always definite enough to answer.

Throughout, I have minimized scholarship, or citations and
surveys of related results. The chapter-by-chapter reviews under
Background and Sources are meant to fill that gap.

I have written for four audiences. One is myself. Having thought about
the Paradox of Voting on and off for many years, discovered many of
the results reported here, been annoyed by repeated misstatements of
important assumptions and findings, worked as a teacher to simplify
arguments and recycle them as much as possible, and become ever
more aware of cycles as a source of coherence, I naturally wished to set
a lot of it down on paper to see what it all looked like. What I saw
required refinement and inspired new findings.

Another intended audience is the community of social-choice
specialists – or if they are not a real community, it may be because
they could never agree on how to reach collective decisions. Their
specific interests often differ from mine, but they can see immediately –
and appreciate, I hope – where I have filled gaps, simplified proofs, found

fault with familiar interpretations, and most of all extended knowledge. I expect some of them to challenge things I have said but hope some will feel challenged to apply and extend those things.

Then there are scholars and scientists who know something of my subject and talk about it from time to time, interpreting and applying its findings, but are not narrow specialists. I have tried to please them with a combination of succinctness, light technical demands, and applications to an array of independently interesting phenomena. At the risk of rudeness, I have also tried to correct them. For it is mostly they who, unwittingly, spread error, among themselves and to their own wider audiences.

The final audience consists of students but also of accomplished scholars and scientists who are merely aware of my subject and face a common conundrum: they wonder if that subject is worth the effort to learn about it, but the only way to find out is to learn about it. I have tried to help them by covering more content in less space with less apparatus but more attention to applications than any other book on the mathematical theory of voting and social choice. To gratify all four audiences – even myself, when I set out to assemble all these pieces about two years ago – I have striven to sprinkle the story of cycles and their sources and consequences with surprises.

I Condorcet's Two Discoveries

Yes, two, the first a prelude to the Paradox of Voting. Both come from his 1785 *Essai* and show, in different ways, how democratic electoral choices can flout the preferences of majorities. Sweeping generalizations of the Paradox appear in later chapters, but right away you will see that cycles are not at all peculiar to majority rule or even voting – but also that majority rule itself and the cycles it generates are peculiarly noteworthy.

I.I THE REJECTION OF CONDORCET WINNERS

Suppose voters are divided into three minority factions, who rank three candidates in order of preference thus:

Liberals	Moderates	Conservatives
Libby	Maude	Connie
Maude	Libby and Connie	Maude
Connie	in either order	Libby

If Liberals are the largest faction and everyone votes for his favorite, Libby wins under Plurality Rule: she has the most votes. But a majority (Moderates and Conservatives) prefer Maude to Libby, and for that matter another majority prefer Maude to Connie. So Plurality Rule can reject a candidate preferred to all others by majorities. We call such a candidate the *Condorcet winner* – even when he loses.

The rejection of Condorcet winners happens with fair frequency when elections between two major parties give way to three-party contests. In the 1970 election for US Senator from New York, Conservative James Buckley won with a plurality, not a majority,

8

defeating both the Democratic candidate and the Republican incumbent, Charles Goodell, who was the Condorcet winner: he occupied Maude's position. Then within a year, Socialist Salvador Allende received a 36 percent plurality for President of Chile, where the Condorcet winner was Christian Democrat Radomiro Tomic. Because Allende's total was less than 40 percent, the final choice was up to Congress, where the conservative Nationalists were willing to support Tomic. Alas, the Christian Democrats voted with the Socialists for Allende on the principle that the plurality favorite, not the Condorcet winner, is the true popular choice. In New York, Senator Buckley quickly restored two-party competition by joining the Republicans. In Chile, President Allende quickly broke his promise to the Christian Democrats to govern constitutionally. You know the rest.

This problem – if it is one – is not peculiar to Plurality Rule. The Double-Vote Rule, which requires a runoff when no candidate receives a majority of votes, might choose Maude. But maybe not: a runoff might pit Libby against Connie. A runoff would have bypassed Goodell and Tomic, each of whom had the fewest votes. Popular among social-choice theorists are the Borda and Approval Rules. The former chooses the candidate with the greatest Borda score, got by finding his rank from the bottom (0, 1, 2, etc.) in each voter's preference ordering and summing those ranks across all voters. Let five voters rank three candidates as follows:

	1	2	3	4	5	Borda scores:
2	x	x	x	y	y	$x = 6$
1	y	y	y	z	z	$y = 7$
0	z	z	z	x	x	$z = 2$

Then y has the greatest Borda score though x is the Condorcet winner. Like Plurality Rule, Approval Rule picks the candidate with the most votes, but it allows each voter to vote for (to "approve") more than one candidate. In that same example, if every voter votes for his first and second choices, y wins and the Condorcet winner is again rejected.

I.2 THE PARADOX OF VOTING

Once we have preferential ballots, ones that rank candidates in order of preference, we can spot and choose any Condorcet winner. But that does no good if there is no Condorcet winner to spot, as in Condorcet's second example, the Paradox of Voting:

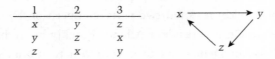

Here a majority (voters 1 and 3) prefer x to y, another (1 and 2) y to z, and a third (2 and 3) z to x. As depicted, the relation of majority preference is *cyclic*. Not only is there no Condorcet winner (that can happen when two candidates are tied), but every possible choice is *unstable* under majority rule: whichever candidate is chosen, some majority prefers a different choice.

Cycles are not limited to three voters or candidates. Assume any number n of voters. So long as $3 \le n \ne 4$, we can always divide them into three minority factions and assign them Condorcet's three preference orderings, one to each faction. Because each of the three is a minority, any two make a majority. So it is still true that majorities prefer x to y, y to z, and z to x. And instead of three candidates, assume *three or more alternatives*, however many and of whatever sort you please. Let them include x and y, but now let z be the *set* of all the rest. Then majorities still prefer x to y, but now y to every alternative in z and each of the latter to x – an all-inclusive cycle.

Our symmetric 3×3 picture might suggest that cycles make the social choice a matter of indifference: it matters not what is chosen. But consider another example:

1	2	3
x	y	u
y	z	z
z	w	w
w	x	x
u	u	y

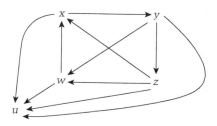

We again have a cycle, indeed two inside a third. But certainly we can reject u, to which a majority prefers everything else, and maybe w, which is Pareto inefficient: everyone prefers z to w.

Those examples are purely abstract, but a concrete case of cycles and instability arises whenever a pizza is divided by majority vote among three diners, each a slice maximizer. Then a majority prefers $(1/2, 1/2, 0)$ to $(1/3, 1/3, 1/3)$, but majorities also prefer $(2/3, 0, 1/3)$ to $(1/2, 1/2, 0)$, $(0, 1/3, 2/3)$ to $(2/3, 0, 1/3)$, and $(1/2, 1/2, 0)$ to $(0, 1/3, 2/3)$ – a cycle. Those four divisions are not exhaustive, of course, but any division (X, Y, Z) must be unstable: at least one slice, say X, exceeds zero, ensuring that a majority prefers $(0, Y + X/2, Z + X/2)$ to (X, Y, Z).

1.3   WHAT THE PARADOX MEANS AND DOES NOT

What may seem paradoxical, impossible but true, is that majority preferences can form a cycle although majorities are made up of individuals whose shared preferences are quite unremarkable. Condorcet's very example reveals the solution: the preferences for x to y, y to z, and z to x are those of three different majorities with no member in common (a common member would have to have a most remarkable preference).

Beyond that, the immediate lesson of Condorcet's two examples is that popular voting rules can produce unpopular choices (compared with alternatives), a result that is sometimes avoidable (first example) and sometimes not (second). If our goal is to elect the most popular candidate, or one of several, and if majority preference is the criterion of relative popularity, then it may seem obvious that we ought to reject any candidate to whom a majority prefers another. But this assumes there always exists a most popular candidate by that criterion. Condorcet's second example proves there does not.

The academic notoriety of that example suggests something worse. Like a grotesque deformity that fascinates as it appalls, commanding our attention more firmly the harder we try in our embarrassment to look away, the Paradox of Voting has drawn endless scrutiny with reactions of discomfiture if not opprobrium. A cycle of majority preferences has seemed to many to be either an antinomy to be solved, necessarily by uncovering a false assumption or flawed inference, or else a misfortune to be banned or bypassed if possible and regretted if not. But why? Cycles are facts. They happen – quite often, we shall see – and I have never heard of them hurting anyone. Whatever is chosen, some majority is disappointed. But that is true of the first, cycle-free example too. It is just that if Maude is chosen, the disappointed majority (Liberals plus Conservatives) cannot agree on a better choice. In either case, it is not as though "*the* majority" is disappointed. Do cycles block choices? No, all voting rules make choices even when cycles are present, and the familiar ones sometimes reject Condorcet winners even when they are available – a fact well known to the champions of those rules.

An old challenge to cyclic *individual* preferences should apply, if at all, to cyclic majority preferences too. Say you prefer x to y to z to x, and you choose x from among those three alternatives – quite arbitrarily, perhaps. Then, runs the argument, you should be willing to pay something to change that choice to z, then something more to choose y, next even more to choose x again, and so on round the cycle – to act as a money pump. But why? Why pay for z to begin with if you like y more? The underlying assumption is that he who demands payment can keep changing your set of feasible alternatives, first from $\{x, y, z\}$ to $\{x, z\}$, then to $\{y, z\}$, etc. But if so, you would soon realize that you were choosing in effect from $\{x, y, z\}$. And if, faced with the cycle, you were equally willing to choose any one of those three alternatives, you would pay nothing for any of them. Otherwise, you might be willing to pay, but only once for only one.

Some scholars have called cycles "inconsistent," "incoherent," "meaningless," and "illogical," as though they were self-contradictory or nonsensical assertions rather than events that sometimes occur. Maybe all they mean is that cycles (or their descriptions) contradict some plausible assumption or expected pattern. But that is true of every surprising discovery. With the literal meanings of those epithets lost, only their pejorative connotations remain. We are told that cycles are bad. We are not told why.

Because majority rule is so often used to make pairwise social choices, one might proffer majority preference as the criterion of better-to-worse for society. Then the Paradox of Voting shows that a best choice is not always possible, that every feasible choice is worse than some other. That in turn has three notable consequences. One is that social welfare is not a maximand, something that can always be maximized. Another is that societies (and other groups that act by voting) cannot always be modeled anthropomorphically, as classically rational persons choosing what is best for themselves. A third is that political outcomes are harder to explain and predict than one may have fancied: if majorities are empowered to do anything they wish but their preferences form a cycle, then every possible outcome appears to be opposed by a group empowered to block it. More consequences, and more surprising ones, will show up in Chapters 7–10. But a surprise is not evidence of error or misfortune, and an intellectually challenging one is not an obstacle to thought but a reason to think. As it happens, Condorcet's examples have prompted a great deal of enjoyable reflection that has led to deeper findings and creative proposals.

1.4 WHY MAJORITIES: MAY'S THEOREM

Condorcet was a champion of majority rule, but his two discoveries show that it is not always clear what that means when the feasible alternatives are three or more. It is clear enough when they are only two, of course. Then one is chosen – it *beats* the other, let us say – if and only if a simple majority of nonabstainers prefer it, or say they do by voting for it. But what is so special about majority preferences, or two-alternative majority rule? A famous answer comes from May (1954).

Under any two-alternative voting rule, each voter votes for one alternative or abstains (maybe out of indifference), and the outcome is one of the two alternatives or a tie (no decision). What properties should the rule have? May suggests three (which I have simplified a bit):

> *Anonymity.* Switching the votes of any two voters leaves the outcome unchanged.
>
> *Neutrality.* Reversing every vote reverses the outcome unless it was a tie.
>
> *Fragility of Ties.* If, following a tie, some erstwhile abstainers now vote for x, all else staying the same, then x is the new outcome.

Anonymity requires equal treatment of voters: if the outcome changes when two voters switch votes, the rule must be biased in favor of the voter who likes the change. Neutrality requires equal treatment of alternatives: if one alternative is chosen and remains chosen after all votes are reversed, the procedure must be biased in favor of that alternative. Fragility of Ties makes ties rare: they cannot persist in the face of new information that tilts the balance in one direction.

Obviously, majority rule – or simple-majority rule, to be exact – has all three properties. May's Theorem is that it alone does. For if we assume all three, we can deduce

> *Majority Rule.* x beats y if there are more x votes than y votes, and they tie if there are just as many.

To see why, consider the two cases that can arise.

Case 1. There are just as many x as y votes. If we switch one x vote with one y vote, next another x vote with another y vote, and so on until all x or y votes are exhausted, the outcome stays the same according to Anonymity. But because there are just as many x as y votes, the overall effect is a reversal of every vote, ensuring that the outcome does not stay the same, according to Neutrality, unless it was a tie. So a tie it must have been.

Case 2. There are more x votes than y votes. Say there are k more. Then if we replace k of the x votes by abstentions, x ties y according to Case 1. So restoring those votes makes x the new outcome, hence the original outcome, thanks to Fragility of Ties.

Conclusion: Simple-majority rule is the one and only two-alternative voting rule that is anonymous, neutral, and tie-fragile. In a way, any other rule is not a pure or complete voting rule: if it violates Fragility of Ties, it ignores some voting information, and if it violates Anonymity or Neutrality, it reflects some nonvoting information – information about differences between voters or alternatives. "Beat" relations other than majority preference can be cyclic too, but majority cycles will play the starring role in the story of cycles. May's Theorem explains why.

1.5   MORE THAN CYCLES: McGARVEY'S THEOREM

Majority preferences can be cyclic, of course, but is there any other relational pattern that they always fit or flout? Obviously, they are *asymmetric*: if x is the majority preferred to y, then y cannot be to x. But beyond that, majority preferences can take any form whatever. So before generalizing the Paradox of Voting beyond majority rule, let us assume majority rule and generalize beyond cycles to every possible asymmetric relational pattern.

Given any combination of preference orderings, one for each voter, I have portrayed the corresponding relation of majority preference with a *digraph,* a set of arrows and alternatives in which every arrow joins exactly two alternatives and any two alternatives are joined by at most one arrow. But we can also do the reverse: start with *any* digraph G, in effect any asymmetric relation, and find a combination of preference orderings (a possible society) whose relation of majority preference is portrayed by G. For that, we need more voters than alternatives but only four times more. To be exact: if G is any digraph comprising $k \geq 2$ alternatives, there exist orderings $\Omega_1, \ldots, \Omega_{4k}$ of those k alternatives such that G contains $x \to y$, or x beats y according to G, when and only when the number of "voters" who prefer x to y (the number of indices i for which x is above y in Ω_i) exceeds the number who prefer y to x.

This theorem, from McGarvey (1953), is obviously true when $k = 2$. I shall show that *if* it is true *for any given* k, then it must be true as well for $k + 1$. It follows that the theorem is true for $k = 3$, $k = 4$, and so on, hence for all k (by "mathematical induction," as we say).

In $G - x$, the result of deleting any x from G, let B be an ordering of those alternatives (if any) that *beat* x according to G, T an ordering of those that *tie* x, and N an ordering of those that are *beaten by* x. Let B^{-1} be the inverse of B (same alternatives in opposite order), T^{-1} that of T, and N^{-1} that of N. By inductive hypothesis, there are orderings $\Omega_1, \ldots, \Omega_{4k}$ for which $G - x$ portrays the corresponding majority preferences. Here is the promised $4(k + 1)$-fold combination of orderings for which G portrays the majority preferences:

						x			
x		x				N^{-1}	N^{-1}	B	B
Ω_1	...	Ω_{2k}	Ω_{2k+1}	...	Ω_{4k}	T^{-1}	T^{-1}	x	T
	x			x		B^{-1}	B^{-1}	T	x
							x	N	N

Between alternatives other than x, the $G - x$ pattern, which also is the G pattern, is preserved: the four added orderings have no effect on majority preferences because every individual preference is offset by an opposite one, so only the first $4k$ count. But those $4k$ and also the next two have no effect on x because the number of preferences for x over everything else equals the number for everything else over x. So only the last two orderings affect x, and they ensure the desired G pattern: for all b in B, n in N, and t in T, G has $b \to x \to n$ but neither $t \to x$ nor $x \to t$.

McGarvey's Theorem will let us illustrate complicated patterns of majority preference in later chapters by showing digraphs alone, not backed by voter preferences.

I do not know if that theorem is peculiar to simple-majority rule. I do know it cannot be extended very far. Suppose that x beats y only if three-quarters of voters prefer x to y. Then we cannot have $x \to y \to z \to x$, for if three-quarters prefer x to y and likewise y to z, then at least half prefer x to z.

1.6   BEYOND MAJORITY RULE: WARD'S THEOREM

Let us not give too much deference to majority preference. Even democracies often deviate from majority rule, or May's three properties. Start with Anonymity. It is violated, of course, by rules that weight voters unequally, as in shareholder elections, but also by the vaunted Westminster system of district voting to elect one of two parties to control a legislature. Let there be three districts, each with three voters, who vote for parties x and y as follows:

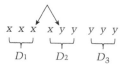

If two votes are switched as shown, the outcome changes from y to x, contrary to Anonymity. Or if we reinterpret x and y as two versions of a bill and D_1 and D_2 as two legislative houses, then the reverse switch changes the outcome from x to a tie, or deadlock. In both cases, the new outcome is opposed by an overall majority. Under the Westminster system, the victor need win only a bare majority of votes in a bare majority of districts. That is little more than a quarter of all votes if districts are equal in voting population, leaving almost three-quarters opposed to the outcome. Less extreme cases arise with fair frequency. In 1996 and again in 2012, Democrats won a majority of votes for the US House of Representatives, Republicans a majority of seats.

Or consider Neutrality. It is violated by any rule that gives an advantage to a default alternative, often the status quo; call it q. Take the two-thirds majority rule used in legislatures for such things as constitutional amendments. If half the legislators favor proposal x and the other half oppose x, then q wins. But if every vote is reversed, q still wins. Neutrality is violated too by the legislative variant of simple-majority rule: it avoids ties by picking default q when voters are equally divided.

The Westminster system violates not only Anonymity but Fragility of Ties. Consider four five-voter districts:

$$\underbrace{xxx\_\_}\quad \underbrace{xxx\_\_}\quad \underbrace{yyy\_\_}\quad \underbrace{yyy\_\_}$$

There is a tie, but filling all those blanks (abstentions) with x would not break it.

So, yes, of course, democracies often use majority rule, but most often in a qualified or compound way, where the overall effect can be far from majoritarian. That effect can still be cyclic, however. In the Paradox of Voting, x beats y, y beats z, and z beats x under majority rule. For the qualified and compound procedures found in real democracies, we cannot assume that x beats y whenever a majority prefers x to y. But in most cases, following Ward (1960), we can make the weaker assumption:

VU x beats y whenever $n - 1$ voters prefer x to y (*Virtual Unanimity*)

where n is still and always the number of voters. In Condorcet's example, $n - 1 = 2$, so **VU** implies that x beats y, y beats z, and z beats x again. But for a cycle, we do not need $n = 3$. It is enough that any $n \geq 3$ voters have the following preferences among as many alternatives:

1	2	.	.	.	i	.	.	.	n
x_1	x_2				x_i				x_n
x_2	x_3				x_{i+1}				x_1
.	.				.				.
.	.				.				.
.	.				.				.
x_{i-1}	x_i				x_n				.
x_i	.				x_1				.
.	.				.				.
.	.				.				.
.	x_n				.				.
x_n	x_1				x_{i-1}				x_{n-1}

For each $j < n$, every voter prefers x_j to x_{j+1} unless x_{j+1} is atop his preference ordering, that is, unless he is voter $j +1$. And all but voter 1 prefer x_n to x_1. So by **VU**, x_1 beats x_2, x_2 beats x_3, and so on down to x_n, which beats x_1 – an n-fold cycle.

Later we shall see how to make even weaker assumptions and derive smaller cycles. For now, notice that if any two nonadjacent alternatives in the cycle are related as beater to beaten, in either direction and for whatever reason, then the big cycle contains a smaller one. Notice too that it is often reasonable to strengthen **VU** so it says, for some $k > 1$, that x beats y whenever $n - k$ voters prefer x to y. Then we need only n/k alternatives and n/k columns, each the preference ordering of k voters.

1.7   INDIVIDUAL RIGHTS: SEN'S PARADOX

Although many democratic procedures that flout majority rule fulfill the weaker **VU**, not all do. Modern democracies constrain outcomes to respect individual rights. If the choice of x over y would violate someone's right to free speech or a fair trial, then y beats x under the US Constitution even if everyone else prefers x to y. But individual rights, too, can generate cycles. According to Nobel Laureate Amartya Sen's celebrated Liberal Paradox of 1970, cycles can occur when any one or two individuals have the right to dictate the social choice between any two alternatives that differ only in their private behavior. In Sen's famous example, a public library has one copy of a pornographic book that no one but Messrs. Lewd and Prude wishes to read, but both of them have intrusive preferences: Lewd most prefers that Prude reads the book (P), next that he himself reads it (L), then that no one reads it (N), whereas Prude prefers N to P to L. Because L and N differ only in Lewd's private behavior and he prefers L to N, L beats N. Similarly, N beats P thanks to Prude's preference. But because both prefer P to L, P beats L – a cycle.

Scholars have wasted disgraceful amounts of time and other resources looking for flaws in Sen's delightful but needlessly contentious example. One need only assume that people have the right to keep or alienate their own property and to make enforceable contracts to do so. Put Crusoe and Friday in a position to exchange a coconut for a banana. Naturally, Crusoe most prefers keeping his coconut while receiving Friday's banana ($\bar{c}b$) and least prefers giving up the coconut but receiving no banana ($c\bar{b}$), whereas Friday most prefers $c\bar{b}$ and least prefers $\bar{c}b$. Mutual gains from trade are possible, however: both prefer an exchange (cb) to the status quo ($\bar{c}\bar{b}$). Because Crusoe prefers $\bar{c}\bar{b}$ to $c\bar{b}$ and those outcomes differ solely in the disposition of his own property, $\bar{c}\bar{b}$ beats $c\bar{b}$. Similarly, $\bar{c}\bar{b}$ beats $\bar{c}b$, $\bar{c}b$ and $c\bar{b}$ both beat cb, and cb beats $\bar{c}\bar{b}$ – another cycle. Here is the picture:

Crusoe	Friday
$\bar{c}b$	$c\bar{b}$
cb	cb
$\bar{c}\bar{b}$	$\bar{c}\bar{b}$
$c\bar{b}$	$\bar{c}b$

Never mind nosey Lewd and Prude: cyclic social preferences based on individual rights are as common as trade.

You may have noticed that this example is a prisoners' dilemma game, a cooperation problem of the simplest sort: each of two players is free to cooperate (C) or defect (D), to trade or not, and each would rather defect regardless of what the other does, yet both prefer mutual cooperation (CC) to mutual defection (DD). So if players have the right to choose, then DD beats CD because player 1 has that preference, and CD beats CC thanks to 2. But if 1 and 2 can solve their dilemma by making a binding contract to cooperate, then CC beats DD. Enforce cooperation in a prisoners' dilemma with rights to choose and you have a cycle.

Not that all cycles based on individual rights involve cooperation. Suppose Crusoe and Friday each has the right to paint his house as he pleases and both prefer blue and yellow to all other colors but Crusoe prefers matching colors, Friday contrasting colors. Then Crusoe prefers BB to YB, outcomes that differ only in the color of his own house, so BB beats YB. Similarly, YB beats YY, which beats BY, which completes the cycle by beating BB. Structurally, this example is no more than a 2 × 2 game without Nash equilibrium. To generalize, take any game without Nash equilibrium. So long as each player has the right to choose any of the strategies open to him (they might include, for example, buying a house but not burglarizing one), we have a social-preference cycle based on individual rights.

Groups have rights too, rights that underlie similar cycles. Just replace Crusoe and Friday in that last example by two adjacent neighborhood or condominium associations. What makes the Paradox of Voting a bit more surprising than everyday games without Nash equilibria is not that majorities are groups: players are often interpreted as groups, such as warring nations or competing teams, firms, or parties. It is that majorities are overlapping groups. That makes it impossible for them to have strictly opposed preferences: one majority cannot prefer BB to BY while another prefers BY to BB. What Condorcet discovered, however, is that three overlapping groups can have something like the conflicting preferences of two persons or disjoint groups: instead of a two-alternative "cycle" (one group prefers x to y, another y to x), we can have a three-alternative cycle.

1.8 A WORD ABOUT WORDS

I have been introducing concepts and labels piecemeal, often in connection with examples. Let me now pull those of recurring importance together in a more general and explicit way.

Despite the likes of Crusoe and Friday, I shall continue to refer to Messrs. 1, 2, ..., n as voters and to speak of social preference and choice although the society in question had but two members. So *voters* are any individuals (or even organized subgroups) who participate in social-choice processes by expressing their preferences, and *social* choices are those made by any committee, community, or other collectivity.

Any social-choice procedure, democratic or not, vote based or not, determines a *social-preference relation*, that of beater to beaten in pairwise contests: x *beats* y if the procedure would choose x, not y, when they alone were feasible. The absence of social preference in either direction is a *tie*. In a *cyclic* social preference, or simply a *cycle*, a beaten path runs from every x to every y: x beats something, which beats something else, and so on down to y.

Instability comes from cycles, of course, but not always and not only. It depends also on the set of feasible alternatives and the prevailing procedure. A *stable* choice from a set is unbeaten by any other member of that set. Suppose the set consists of x, y, and z and they form a cycle: x beats y, y beats z, and z beats x. Then whatever is chosen is *unstable*: another feasible alternative beats it. If we add a fourth feasible alternative that beats the other three, then it alone is stable. Or if we add a fifth that ties the fourth and beats the rest, then both are stable. But if we subtract all but x and z, then z is now stable. Under some procedures, the chosen alternative can be unstable even if another feasible alternative is stable. That happened in Condorcet's first example. For x beats y under Plurality Rule if a majority prefers x to y. So Maude beat Libby and Connie: she alone was stable. But Plurality Rule chose Libby.

A cycle ensures that every alternative is unstable, or beaten by another, in at least one potential feasible set, the cycle itself. The converse is true too, at least for finite, nonempty sets: if every member is beaten by another, there must be a cycle. *Proof.* List the set's members in any order and let x_0 be the first on the list, x_1 the first that beats x_0, x_2 the first that beats x_1, and so on. Because every member is beaten by another and the set is finite, the series x_0, x_1, x_2, ... must have a repetition: some x_i is beaten by x_{i+1}, which is beaten by x_{i+2}, and so on down to x_i itself again – a cycle.

2 Incidence of the Paradox

How common or exotic are cycles and instability? Which patterns of voter preference produce or prevent them? Some deductive results suggest that the cycle-prone patterns are rare, others that they abound. Although well-known results of the latter sort have been over-interpreted, in the end we must conclude that the Paradox of Voting is far from exotic. It is here that I discuss stability in one dimension, its breakdown in two or more, issue packaging, and the misuse of observational evidence.

2.1 BLACK'S MEDIAN-STABILITY THEOREM

Our original, cycle-free example, with Condorcet winner Maude, fits a familiar pattern of voter preference, one based on ideology. Following the groundbreaking 1948 paper of Duncan Black, let any number of alternatives be ordered left to right along a line, and assume that each of n voters likes them less the farther they lie to the left of his favorite alternative or to its right. Nothing need be assumed about preferences *between* left and right. To simplify discussion, let n be odd. Then if we move a finger left to right along the line, we must eventually find the *median favorite*: fewer than half the voters have their favorite alternatives on its left or on its right. Black's Theorem is that *the median favorite is the Condorcet winner*: under majority rule, it beats every other alternative.

Proof. If we locate voters on the line at their favorite alternatives, then fewer than half of them end up left (right) of the median. So the median voters plus those on their right (left) are a majority, and of course they prefer the median favorite to every alternative on its left (right). Because this applies to any nonempty set of alternatives, it applies to any nonempty *subset* of it: it too contains a Condorcet winner. That blocks cycles, which contain none.

In case *n* is even, there could be two median favorites: fewer than half the voters have their favorite alternatives on the left of both or on the right of both. As before, they beat every alternative on the left of both and on their right, but they themselves are tied. So both are stable, or unbeaten, though not Condorcet winners. Cycles are still blocked.

Black's assumption about ideological positions and preferences is called *Single Peakedness* because, when we interpret height on page as degree of preference, that assumption gives every voter a single-peaked preference curve over Black's left-to-right line, as in this picture of our original example:

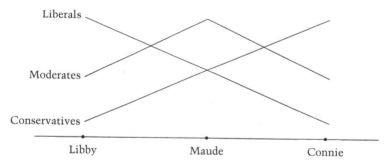

One curve portrays Moderates as indifferent between Libby and Connie, but that is inessential: we can bias any of them toward Libby or Connie by tilting their curves right or left; they are still single peaked.

If we reorder the candidates along the line by switching Maude and Connie, the Liberal curve is no longer single peaked. But Black's assumption still holds, and the *combination of preferences* is still called single peaked, because *some* horizontal lineup makes all preference curves single peaked. Not so in the Paradox of Voting, as shown by these unsuccessful attempts to fit the preference curves of voters 1, 2, and 3 to some horizontal lineup:

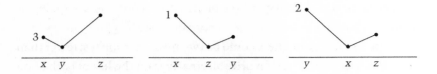

2.2 GENERALIZATIONS OF SINGLE PEAKEDNESS

Single Peakedness has many generalizations, weaker assumptions that still imply stability. The most general of the known ones, a trivial consequence of each of the others, is *Condorcet Freedom*: no three voters have the preference orderings *xyz*, *yzx*, and *zxy*, interpreted so that one adjacent pair in each ordering (e.g. *xy* in *xyz*) *may* be an indifference rather than a preference, as long as it is also *someone's* preference. This assumption excludes any combination of preferences containing Condorcet's original pattern, broadened to allow some indifferences. Having allowed indifference, we must construe a *majority* to mean more than half of those who are *not* indifferent.

Actually, Condorcet Freedom – hence any stronger assumption, such as Single Peakedness – implies more than stability, or the absence of cycles. It implies that *majority preference is transitive*: if majorities prefer *x* to *y* and *y* to *z*, then a majority prefers *x* to *z*.

Proof. Assume on the contrary that no majority prefers *x* to *z*. Then among *concerned voters*, ones who are not indifferent between all three alternatives, more than half like *x* at least as much as *y*, more than half like *y* at least as much as *z*, and at least half like *z* at least as much as *x*. But if more than half of any set belong to one category and at least half to another, some member belongs to both. Among concerned voters, therefore, three must have the preference orderings *xyz*, *yzx*, and *zxy*, with at most one possible indifference in each ordering (because those three voters are concerned). So they prefer *x* to *z*, *y* to *x*, and *z* to *y*. But because majorities do not, some three voters must have the reverse preferences: *z* to *x*, *x* to *y*, and *y* to *z*. So Condorcet Freedom is flouted.

Apart from the qualification about voter indifference, to find a restriction on preference patterns that rules out Condorcet's original pattern and any other that generates cycles, we can do no better than to rule out Condorcet's original pattern. But of course, it is Black's less general restriction that has enough intuitive bite to be plausible, and to make stability plausible, in many cases.

2.3 MORE DIMENSIONS AND 360 DEGREE MEDIANHOOD: COX'S THEOREM

If we strengthen Black's restriction one way and then relax it another, we arrive at the *general spatial model of voting*, where we can re-use his median-stability theorem ironically: to gainsay stability. Assume again that n is odd. The strengthening equates the feasible alternatives with all the points on a line, a "space" of one dimension. For relaxation, we then let them be all the points in a space of *one or more* dimensions. If more than one, they represent different issues that admit of left-to-right positions (guns and butter, social and economic conservatism, or whatnot). As in Black's one-dimensional case, each voter i has a favorite point, V_i, and likes other points less the farther they lie from V_i in any given direction. More specifically, each voter has an *indifference map* consisting of his favorite point girt by *indifference contours*, infinitely many of them, so many so placed that every point lies on exactly one of them. In two dimensions, indifference contours are circles, ellipses, and other shapes, as in this partial picture:

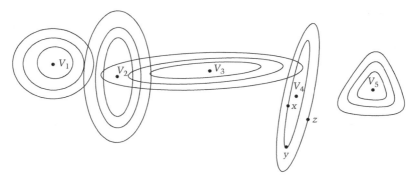

In general, they are the *boundaries of strictly convex sets*. Each voter is indifferent between points on the same indifference contour and prefers points on higher (inner) contours to ones on lower (outer) contours. So voter 4 is indifferent between x and y and prefers both to z.

   In two or more dimensions, there still exist lines, but now infinitely many rather than one, and Black's theorem still applies to them. Let us say that voter i *kisses* line L at point x if either $x = V_i$ or else i has an indifference contour tangent to L at x. In this picture, voter 1 kisses L at V_1, 2 and 3 at y, and 4 at w:

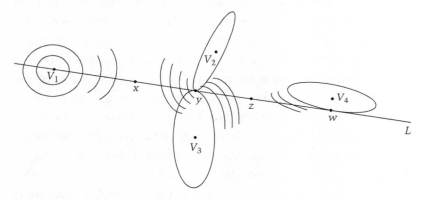

Obviously, each voter kisses any given line at some point and some line at any given point, and he likes points on the line less the farther they lie to the left of his kiss point or to its right. Thus, voter 1 prefers V_1 to x to y to z to w, voter 2 prefers y to x to V_1 and also y to z to w, and so on. We may invoke Black's stability theorem and conclude that the median kiss point on L beats every other point on L under majority rule. It follows, thanks to Cox (1987), that a point x is stable in the whole space only if x is a *360 degree median*, a median kiss point on every line through x – else the median on some line beats x.

   The 360 Degree Medianhood is of interest as a necessary condition for stability because in two or more dimensions it pretty much ensures that *no point is stable*, or unbeaten: were there such a point, say x, then however much we rotated a line at x we would never find kiss points of more than $n/2$ voters on either side of x. This negative result is no more than Black's positive theorem applied to lines drawn in a multi-dimensional space: precisely because the unbeaten point on a line is the median favorite (or kiss point) on that line, an unbeaten point in a space of two dimensions or more would have to be the median favorite on *all* lines through it. The difference is that the median favorite on one line necessarily exists, whereas a point that remains the median favorite as the line is rotated 360 degrees could exist but almost certainly does not.

2.4   PAIRWISE SYMMETRY: PLOTT'S THEOREM

That result contains, in effect, Plott's groundbreaking instability theorem of 1967. Let us say that two voters *kiss each other* at x if they have indifference contours that are tangent and convex to each other at x, or equivalently, that they kiss a line at x but from opposite directions, as in this picture:

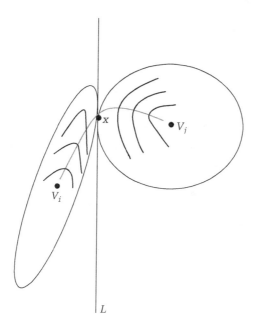

Note that all the kiss points of voters i and j make up their *contract curve*, as in an Edgeworth box. Call x *pairwise symmetric* if voters whose favorite points are not x can be paired one to one so that each kisses his mate at x. For simplicity, let the dimensions be two. Assuming that x is at most one voter's favorite point, Plott proved that x *is unbeaten* (stable) *under majority rule only if* (what is not likely to be true of any point) x *is pairwise symmetric.*

To see why, suppose x is *not* pairwise symmetric. Then some voter has no potential mate to kiss at x or several have too few. Either way, some one or more voters must kiss a line L at x while fewer (maybe none) kiss them back (or kiss L at x in the opposite direction), as in the first of these pictures:

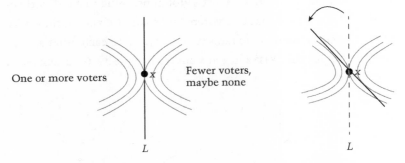

Without loss of generality, suppose that the voters, if any, who kiss L above x are at least as numerous as those who kiss L below. Now rotate L, but ever so slightly. Make the rotation small enough that voters who had kissed L above x still do. But however small the rotation, those who had too few potential mates to kiss at x now kiss the rotated line above x, while those, if any, who had too many now kiss it below x. As a result, more than n/2 voters now kiss that line above x: x is not a median kiss point on the rotated line. Consequently, some point beats x.

2.5   DEFAULT STABILITY AND A SIDE TRIP BEYOND MAJORITY RULE

If it takes but a simple majority to pass new legislation, overturning default alternative q – often the status quo – then the stability of q requires that it be a 360 degree median, a hard condition to meet.

But if it takes a two-thirds majority, then by the same reasoning, the stability condition is less demanding. It is that fewer than two-thirds of voters kiss any line through q on one side of q. For the concurrent-majority rule of bi-cameral legislatures, the condition is that no concurrent majority (comprising majorities from both chambers) kiss any line through q on one side of q. Because two-thirds and concurrent majorities are more rare than simple majorities, these stability conditions are easier to meet than 360 Degree Medianhood.

In general, call a set of voters a *passing coalition* if the shared preference of its members is sufficient to change q to any other point, and assume that *only* a passing coalition can ever do that. Then q is *stable*, or unbeaten, if *no passing coalition kiss any line through q on one side of q.* The chance of a stable q increases with the rarity of passing coalitions. But the broth of our abstraction is too thin to let us read very much into that conclusion. One reason is that q can be so unpopular that it is easy to defeat even by a large concurrent majority. Often it is not some familiar old shoe of a status quo, comfortable and serviceable if cracked and scuffed, but a cold bare foot. In a budget vote, for example, the default budget might be no budget at all, and in Thomas Hobbes's unanimous vote to create a Sovereign, it is a "state of war" in which "the life of man is solitary, poor, nasty, brutish, and short." Another reason is that the issue in most legislators' minds often is not whether to replace q but how to replace it.

2.6 ESSENTIAL PACKAGING

Here is a better way to look at the incidence of cycles and instability. Please forgive a true story. In 1977, the US House of Representatives comprised three minorities: rurals, who sought agriculture subsidies but not food stamps ($a\bar{f}$), urbans, who had the opposite objective ($\bar{a}f$), and suburbans, who disliked both measures ($\bar{a}\bar{f}$). So majorities opposed both a and f. But because rurals and urbans both preferred af to $\bar{a}\bar{f}$, they traded votes, rurals supporting f in return for urban support of a. What follows are the preferences of the three minorities and a picture of majority preferences:

Rurals	Urbans	Suburbans
$a\bar{f}$	$\bar{a}f$	$\bar{a}\bar{f}$
af	af	$a\bar{f}$ and $\bar{a}f$
$\bar{a}f$	$\bar{a}\bar{f}$	*(either order)*
$\bar{a}f$	$a\bar{f}$	af

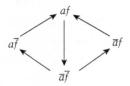

Here we have a double cycle: majorities prefer $\bar{a}\bar{f}$ to $a\bar{f}$, $a\bar{f}$ to af, and af to $\bar{a}f$, but also $\bar{a}f$ to $\bar{a}f$ to af to $\bar{a}\bar{f}$. Historical details are inessential: any vote trade by two minorities who make a majority has the same form and gives rise to cycles.

We can generalize. What is important is not majority rule, two factions, or explicit vote trading, but *essential packaging*: some socially chosen alternative is a package of components that can be chosen together, as a package, but not separately, regardless of whether other components have already been chosen. However many components there may be, we can always divide the package in two, say x and y. It is no great stretch to suppose that those two subpackages, like the aforementioned components, cannot be chosen separately. To reject x is (let us say) to choose $\bar{x}$; likewise y and $\bar{y}$. Because x could not be chosen by itself, in the absence of y, and because y could not be chosen by itself, in the presence of x, $\bar{x}\bar{y}$ beats $x\bar{y}$ and $x\bar{y}$ beats xy. But so long as xy could be chosen as a package in a pairwise contest with $\bar{x}\bar{y}$, it must beat $\bar{x}\bar{y}$, completing another cycle. Yes, this applies not only to legislative packages but to the exchange and prisoners' dilemma examples of Section 1.7. In Section 8.5, I shall generalize more and also show that essential anti-packages – ones whose components can be chosen *only* separately – also require cycles.

2.7   CONTRASTS AND LIMITATIONS, OR PURGING PREPOSTEROUS PREMISES

The essential-package result is important for two reasons. First, although Single Peakedness seems to be true in many cases, so does my assumption of essential packaging – as witness the length and complexity of typical legislation. Maybe both are true often enough to make both stability and instability common occurrences.

Second, although widely celebrated, the spatial instability theorems rest on the false assumption that the feasible alternatives are infinite in number, indeed uncountable. To be feasible, they have to be formulable, in English or some other language, and for that they have to be no longer than some maximum readable length. But that makes them finite in number because there are only finitely many English texts of any given length, however great (yes, legislative texts can mention numbers, e.g. tax rates, but they do so with words or numerals, of which only finitely many are available). This fact is almost always overlooked because the assumption of a preposterously large feasible set does not discredit *positive* stability (or equilibrium or optimality) results, which are far more common than negative ones (which are seen as paradoxical, after all). The reason is that if x is stable (unbeaten) in a big set, it is perforce stable in any smaller subset that contains it. But if x is *un*stable in a big set, it might easily be *stable* in a smaller subset. Letting $\succ$ be any asymmetric relation, the following implication is valid:

$y \succ x$ for no y in big set $\Rightarrow y \succ x$ for no y in small subset.

But its converse is not. The logical fallacy of confusing the two has, I believe, led many to read too much into spatial instability results.

Even so, we can allow the feasible points to be finite in number and still prove that a stable one must be a 360 degree median, provided we assume that they are numerous and dense enough to satisfy this condition:

Whenever a majority M prefers a point x to a feasible point y, there exists a feasible point x′ close enough to x that M also prefers x′ to y.

But on its face that is still highly restrictive, or rather, ever greater density is ever more restrictive, ever less likely to be realized, while of course making instability ever more likely. In many cases, the alternatives we regard as feasible are but a handful – the candidates for office, the motions on the agenda, the coalitions that might form a government, and the like.

In the essential-package case of Section 2.6, I proved instability by constructing a cycle. In the spatial case of Section 2.3, I proved near certain instability without constructing a cycle. *Assuming* instability (plus an extreme restriction on indifference contours, later eliminated by Schofield (1978)), McKelvey (1976) has famously deduced that the underlying cycle must be all-inclusive: every point belongs to it. But that too assumes infinitude.

Spatial instability theorems are instructive, but their important lesson is metatheoretical: they do not so much limit what can be found in reality but what can be proved in principle. Black's theorem about stable medians holds for infinite "spaces" of one dimension. As a positive stability result, it is not impaired by the assumption of infinitude, and originally it was proved without it. A comparable theorem for multi-dimensional spaces, or even convex subspaces, would have this form:

Assuming the spatial model (every voter has an indifference map) for two or more dimensions, there exists an unbeaten point.

The spatial instability results, most dramatically Plott's (about pairwise symmetry), *rule out any such theorem*. What I have added is that Black's theorem already did that by applying to all single lines in multi-dimensional spaces, but with roughly the opposite of its one-dimensional conclusion – not stability but near certain instability.

2.8   OBSERVABLE EVIDENCE OF CYCLES

Instead of assuming and deducing things, can we discover the incidence of cycles by observation? Yes, sometimes, but less often than one might have expected. Suppose the voting population is divided into three minorities, and under Plurality Rule they vote for their favorites. But that is compatible with both of Condorcet's examples, the Liberal–Moderate–Conservative example with its Condorcet winner, and the Paradox of Voting. Votes do not tell us enough to distinguish the two cases. Preferential ballots would, of course, reveal a cycle or Condorcet winner – assuming sincere voting. But they are rarely used.

Legislative votes reveal more information about preferences, but not enough. Let a three-member legislature take two votes. At the first, bill x loses to status quo q, with Rep. 1 voting for x, 2 and 3 against. At the second vote, bill y wins against q, with Reps. 1 and 2 voting for y, 3 against. Assuming that legislators vote their real preferences, we may infer this much, but no more, about those preferences:

Rep. 1 prefers x and y to q,

Rep. 2 prefers y to q to x,

and   Rep. 3 prefers q to x and y.

See the information gap: we do not know 1 or 3's preference between x and y. If both prefer x to y, we have the preference orderings xyq, yqx, and qxy – the Paradox of Voting. If instead either or both prefer y to x, then y is the Condorcet winner. Yes, a third vote, between x and y, would close the gap. But then a defeated bill (x) would be pitted against a victorious one (y). Rarely, if ever, is that allowed. The obstacle to observation is quite general. Assuming again that legislators vote their real preferences, and assuming no ties, no individual indifferences, and no reconsideration of rejected alternatives, I have proved elsewhere that every possible history of pairwise majority votes is compatible with cycles but also with their absence: no possible history contains enough information to distinguish the two cases.

Single Peakedness, alias the One-Dimensional or Ideological Model, may seem at first to be observable. We have little trouble placing politicians in left-to-right order, and for the US Congress ADA scores do that with a certain precision. But all this shows is that each congressman has an ideological average, reckoned from his votes on a selection of conspicuously ideological issues. That is necessarily true, however anyone votes.

Much more consequential is the dimensional analysis of recorded votes by Poole and Rosenthal (1985). Often that fits a single factor or dimension to large chunks of legislative history, and unlike

ADA scores it discovers a single dimension instead of imposing one or even assuming that one exists. Its value comes from locating every legislator at a point whose distance from those of his colleagues tells us how much alike their positions are. That in turn shows how the legislature is divided into congenial clusters, typically parties. But even when this method finds that a single dimension fits votes perfectly, Single Peakedness does not follow.

To see why, suppose that a legislature divided into three factions votes on two mutually exclusive bills, x and y, with q the status quo ante. Suppose faction A, a majority, votes against x while B and C vote for x, and then A and B both vote for y, C against. Following Poole–Rosenthal, the first vote divides the legislature into A and $B + C$, the second vote into $A + B$ and C, together requiring the left-to-right ordering ABC (or the reverse), a perfect fit to one dimension. But look at the preferences revealed by those votes:

> A prefers y to q to x,
> B prefers x and y to q,
> and C prefers x to q to y.

They violate Single Peakedness. If we horizontally order the three alternatives xyq, then C's preference curve is not single peaked. Likewise A's curve with yxq, and B's with xqy. In this case, of course, there is no cycle: because A is a majority, x is the Condorcet winner.

But consider another example, where all three factions are minorities and the story begins with legislators' actual preferences:

> A prefers x to y to q,
> B prefers y to q to x,
> and C prefers q to x to y.

So A alone votes for x, which loses, then A and B vote for y, C against. As before, votes perfectly fit one dimension in the Poole–Rosenthal sense. But this time we know more about preferences than what is revealed by votes. We are given the full preference orderings of all legislators, and they not only violate Single Peakedness but produce a cycle of majority preferences: x to y to q to x. We did not infer that cycle from votes, of course, but that is my point: votes do not reveal whether there is a cycle.

It is one thing to order legislators from left to right, quite another to add alternatives and preference curves. Scholars who work with recorded votes often do not notice this because they do not observe when pairs of alternatives, such as (x, q) and (y, q), overlap, although that was essential to my example. We can generalize: legislative histories that reveal even a modicum of overlap, along with a bit of variation in winning sides, can never satisfy Single Peakedness – so I have proved elsewhere. Poole–Rosenthal have found factors that separate legislators, not legislation: they are not the "issue-dimensions" of the spatial model. No wonder they have proved hard to interpret.

To see what real evidence of cycles might look like, go back to the vote trade between urban and rural congressmen in Section 2.5. Rather than directly reveal the preferences that made up the cycle, the urban and rural minorities simply voted for a and f, singly or as a package. But the winning majority is a majority of minorities, neither of which benefits from both measures. In other words, a and f obviously benefit two different groups, both minorities, proving that af is an *essential package* supported by a majority, hence part of a cycle. More generally, we can follow the money to see if simple laws or simple parts of complex laws benefit only minorities, but ones that together make a majority.

3   Social Rationality

One lesson of the Paradox of Voting is that social-choice procedures sometimes flout social rationality: they do not fulfill the conditions of rationality long assumed for individual choice. The rough idea is that a rational individual always makes a most preferred choice, but a society cannot when the social preference is cyclic. In a way, Arrow's celebrated Impossibility Theorem generalizes this lesson – but not the Paradox of Voting, as is too often alleged. The theorem does show that certain modest assumptions force a breakdown in the transitivity of either social preference or social indifference, the beat or tie relation, but that is consistent with the absence of cycles. Even so, Arrow's Theorem can be turned into a generalization of the Paradox of Voting – we can add a bit to his assumptions and get a cycle. Chapter 4 shows how.

3.1   CHOICE FUNCTIONS AND RATIONALITY

A classically rational actor always chooses a best feasible alternative according to his preference ordering of all possible alternatives. To couch this idea in more exact terms, it is customary to talk about choice functions rather than actors, individual or collective. Take a universe A of mutually exclusive *alternatives*, denoted x, y, etc. Choices are made from finite, nonempty subsets of A, denoted α, β, etc. A rule, procedure, or motivation for doing so can be represented by a function C – a *choice function* – that turns every α into a nonempty subset $C(\alpha)$ of α, the *choice set* from α. Think of $C(\alpha)$ as the set of permissible choices from α, or of those alternatives that a certain subject would be willing to choose from α. C is *rational in the weakest sense* if it is *rationalized* by some relation P on A, an underlying "preference" relation. That means:

For every α, $C(α) = \{x \in α \mid yPx$ for no y in a$\}$ ($C(α)$ comprises the P-best members of any given α).

Assuming as always that $\emptyset \neq C(α) \subseteq α$, rationalizability has four trivial but notable consequences:

Every α has a *P-best member*, a member x such that yPx for no member y (else $C(α)$ would be empty).

P is *asymmetric* and therefore irreflexive: never $xPyPx$ and therefore never xPx (else $\{x, y\}$ or $\{x\}$ would have no P-best member).

P is *acyclic*: never $x_1Px_2P \cdots x_kPx_1$, $k \geq 3$ (else $\{x_1, \ldots, x_k\}$ would have no P-best member).

P is the relation of *pairwise choice*: xPy if and only if $x \neq y$ and $C(\{x, y\}) = \{x\}$ (for "xPy" ensures that y is not a P-best member of $\{x, y\}$, so x must be).

The first consequence is equivalent to the second and third, to asymmetry plus acyclicity. Thanks to the last consequence, any rationalizing relation must be that of pairwise choice. Henceforth, I shall always equate *preference*, or P, with *pairwise choice*, whether or not C is rationalizable.

Having assumed rationality in the weak sense, and with it the *acyclicity* of P, one might strengthen acyclicity to the assumption that P is *transitive* ($xPyPz \Rightarrow xPz$) or – what is stronger – *negatively transitive* (not $-xPy$ & not $-yPz \Rightarrow$ not $-xPz$). Given asymmetry, acyclicity makes P a (strict) *suborder*, transitivity a (strict) *partial ordering*, negative transitivity a (strict) *weak ordering* of A ("strict" means asymmetric). Define *indifference* and *weak preference*:

xIy if and only if not xPy and not yPx.
xRy if and only if not yPx.

Then negative transitivity is tantamount to the transitivity of R, also to that of P and I. Add that to rationalizability and you have *rationality in the strong sense*, rationalizability by a weak ordering. A notable equivalent is the *Weak Axiom of Revealed Preference* (WARP):

Unless $C(\alpha) - \beta$ is empty, it equals $C(\alpha - \beta)$.

Art lovers are bound to admire this summary:

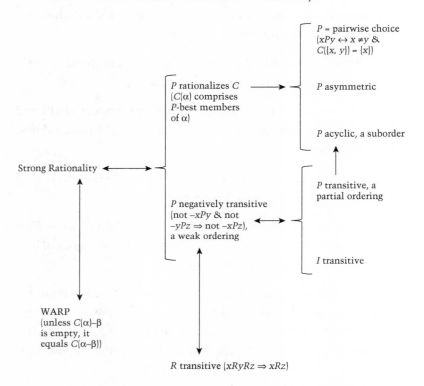

For special purposes, one sometimes assumes *connexity* $(x \neq y \Rightarrow xPy \text{ or } yPx)$, no indifference between distinct alternatives. Combined with asymmetry, that makes acyclicity, transitivity, and negative transitivity equivalent to each other. And combined with asymmetry and acyclicity, it makes P a (strict) *linear ordering* of A. So every linear ordering of A is also a weak ordering, a partial ordering, and a suborder.

Look again at rationality, weak or strong, stated in full as a condition on C:

For some [weak ordering] P and all α, $C(\alpha) = \{x \in \alpha \mid yPx \text{ for no } y \text{ in } \alpha\}$.

Reverse the quantifiers in this requirement and you have *pseudo* rationality:

> For all α and some [weak ordering] P, $C(\alpha) = \{x \in \alpha \mid yPx \text{ for no } y \text{ in } \alpha\}$.

So pseudo rationality allows P to depend on (to vary with) α, but real rationality does not: it fixes P as the pairwise choice relation on A. Because it requires pairwise choice to be acyclic (and, in the strong version, negatively transitive), real rationality is restrictive: not every C is rational. But pseudo rationality is utterly vacuous: every possible C, however goofy, satisfies it. *Proof.* Given α, just let P be the relation of members to nonmembers of $C(\alpha)$.

3.2 RATIONALITY AND THE CLASSICAL FRAMEWORK OF SOCIAL CHOICE

Following Kenneth Arrow's *Social Choice and Individual Values* (1952, 2nd edn 1963), a book that helped win him the Nobel Prize in Economics, the study of social choice is often couched in the following terms: start again with universe A of alternatives, but add a number n of individuals, or *voters*, indexed 1, 2, ..., n and denoted i, j, etc. Let N be the set of them. Let function (or functional) C now depend on voter preferences. It turns certain *preference profiles*, or ordered n-tuples $\mathbf{P} = (P_1, \ldots, P_n)$, $\mathbf{P}' = (P'_1, \ldots, P'_n)$, etc. of weak orderings of A, into choice functions $C_{\mathbf{p}}$, $C_{\mathbf{p}'}$, etc. As always,

$$\varnothing \neq C_{\mathbf{p}}(\alpha) \subseteq \alpha \text{ for all } \alpha.$$

For which profiles $\mathbf{P}$ is $C_{\mathbf{p}}$ defined? All of them, Arrow assumed, but to simplify discussion I shall assume that the domain of C is the family of all ordered n-tuples of *linear* orderings of A.

For any such $\mathbf{P}$, define *social preference*, or $\succ_{\mathbf{p}}$, as *pairwise social choice*, and *social weak preference* and *indifference* in the obvious ways:

> $x \succ_{\mathbf{p}} y$ if and only if $x \neq y$ and $C_{\mathbf{p}}(\{x, y\}) = \{x\}$.
>
> $x \succcurlyeq_{\mathbf{p}} y$ if and only if not $y \succ_{\mathbf{p}} x$.
>
> $x \approx_{\mathbf{p}} y$ if and only if not $x \succ_{\mathbf{p}} y$ and not $y \succ_{\mathbf{p}} x$.

Recall that if C_p is rational, it is rationalized by $\succ_p$, and by $\succ_p$ alone, making $\succ_p$ acyclic. So if C_p is rational in the strong sense – as Arrow assumed – then $\succ_p$ is a weak ordering of A. That property has several noteworthy equivalents. You know three: $\succ_p$ is negatively transitive, $\succcurlyeq_p$ is transitive, and $\succ_p$ and $\approx_p$ are both transitive. Here is a fourth: $x \succ_p y \succcurlyeq_p z \Rightarrow x \succ_p z$.

The most familiar voting rules – Plurality, Double Vote (runoff), Alternative Vote, Approval, Borda – all amount to majority rule when restricted to pairs – when applied to alternatives two at a time. For they all have this consequence:

> $x \succ_p y$ (i.e., $x \neq y$ and $C_p (\{x, y\}) = \{x\}$) if and only if $\{i \mid x P_i y\}$ is bigger than $\{i \mid y P_i x\}$.

In other words, *the familiar voting rules all equate social preference with majority preference.* They diverge in content only when applied to sets of three or more alternatives. But of course, majority preference can be cyclic. So every ordinary voting rule can determine a choice function that flouts even weak rationality: no relation rationalizes it.

It is sometimes believed, on the contrary, that the Borda Rule escapes those "paradoxical" cycles. If this just means that it always chooses something, cycles notwithstanding, then that is true of any and every voting rule. If instead it means that the Borda Rule always gives us a choice function rationalized by the social ordering of alternatives according to their Borda scores, then it is simply false. Applied to α, the Borda Rule does choose those members of α that rank highest in the Borda-score ordering of α. But that ordering depends on and varies with α. Let C_p be the Borda choice function determined by **P**. Then:

> For every α and some weak ordering (Borda ordering) B of α, $C_p(\alpha) = \{x \in \alpha \mid y B x$ for no y in $\alpha\}$.

But thanks to the order of quantifiers, what C_p satisfies is pseudo rationality. Applied to pair sets, Borda agrees with majority rule.

That makes it as susceptible to cycles as any voting rule. To nail the point, let $n = 3$ and suppose in **P** that voter 1 prefers x to y to z, 2 prefers y to z to x, and 3 prefers z to x to y – Condorcet's example. Then if C represents the Borda Rule, we have $C_{\mathbf{p}}(\{x, y, z\}) = \{x, y, z\}$ but also $C_{\mathbf{p}}(\{x, y\}) = \{x\}$, $C_{\mathbf{p}}(\{y, z\}) = \{y\}$, and $C_{\mathbf{p}}(\{z, x\}) = \{z\}$ – a social-preference cycle.

3.3   ARROW'S THEOREM

Arrow's Paradox, or Impossibility Theorem, shows that strong social rationality is blocked by some very modest conditions on n, A, and $\succ$. Actually, it shows a bit more, for the rationalizability of C is not needed – though one of its consequences, the asymmetry of $\succ$, is presupposed. The theorem asserts the inconsistency of five conditions:

A A has three or more members.

U   Every unanimous preference is a social preference: if $x P_i$ y for all i, then $x \succ_{\mathbf{p}} y$ (*Unanimity*, or *Pareto*).

Đ   There is no one whose every preference is perforce the social preference, at least when everyone else disagrees with him: there is no i such that, for all P, x, and y, if xP_i y but $yP_j x$ for every $j \neq i$, then $x \succ_{\mathbf{p}} y$ (*Nondictatorship*).

I   Whether $x \succ_{\mathbf{p}} y$ holds depends on preferences only between x and y: if $x \succ_{\mathbf{p}} y$ and $\mathbf{P}'$ is any xy-twin of **P** (same restrictions to $\{x, y\}$), then $x \succ_{\mathbf{p}'} y$ too (*Independence of Irrelevant Alternatives*).

T $\succ_{\mathbf{p}}$ weakly orders A: $\succ_{\mathbf{p}}$ and $\approx_{\mathbf{p}}$ are both transitive, or equivalently, $x \succ_{\mathbf{p}} y \succcurlyeq_{\mathbf{p}} z \Rightarrow x \succ_{\mathbf{p}} z$ (*Transitivity*).

Arrow originally assumed the rationalizability of $C_{\mathbf{p}}$ (for every **P**) and with it the equation of $\succ_{\mathbf{p}}$ with pairwise social choice. Although not one of the assumptions needed to prove his theorem, that equation sharpens the point of those assumptions. Why assume that social preferences include all unanimous preferences (**U**) or that no one can dictate them all (**Đ**) unless they amount to pairwise *choices*? Also why assume **T** except to make social preference mimic rational individual preference, which is perforce pairwise choice? And then why assume three or more alternatives (**A**) except that otherwise **T** would be vacuously true? As for **I**, Arrow originally couched that assumption in terms of C rather than $\succ$: if **P** and **P′** are α-twins (same restrictions to α), then $C_{\mathbf{P'}}(\alpha) = C_{\mathbf{P}}(\alpha)$. This says that the social choice from any set depends on voter preferences only between members of that set. My $\succ$ version of **I**, Arrow's own later version, simply applies that general assumption to two-member sets, or it does if $\succ_{\mathbf{p}}$ is equated with pairwise social choice. More generally, why care what properties social preference has if, whatever else it may mean, a social preference for x over y does not compel the victory of x over y in a contest between them? The many interpreters of Arrow who forbear to equate social preference with pairwise social choice also forbear to tell us what else that centrally important relation might be.

When $\succ_{\mathbf{p}}$ is interpreted as majority preference, **U**, **Đ**, and **I** are satisfied but **T** is not. The beauty of Arrow's Theorem is that **U**, **Đ**, and **I** vastly relax Majority Rule. Its drawback is that **T** strengthens **Acyclicity**. So **AUĐI** do not generalize the Voting Paradox: they do not imply that $\succ_{\mathbf{p}}$ is ever cyclic. They merely imply that *either* social preference *or* social indifference is sometimes *nontransitive*. Absent a cycle, that never blocks the existence of a stable, or best, or unbeaten choice. Even so, Arrow gave us assumptions and a style of proof that will open doors (in Chapter 4) to similar theorems that do reveal cycles.

3.4 ON INTERPRETING AND MISINTERPRETING THE INDEPENDENCE OF IRRELEVANT ALTERNATIVES

They miss the sweeping generality of **AUĐI** who believe, following a mistake by Arrow himself, that the Borda Rule violates **I**. To recreate that mistake, start with the C version of **I**, and suppose three of five voters prefer x to y to z in **P**, the rest y to z to x. Then $C_\mathbf{p}(\{x, y, z\}) = \{y\}$ but $C_\mathbf{p}(\{x, y\}) = \{x\}$ under the Borda Rule. That is no violation of **I**, however, but of WARP, hence of social rationality. For **I** requires invariance in the social choice when individual preferences change outside the feasible set while the feasible set itself (or the pair of alternatives being compared) *stays the same*. But in the example, individual preferences did not change at all. It was the feasible set that changed (from $\{x, y, z\}$ to $\{x, y\}$). Anyone can err, but it is remarkable that Arrow himself is the author of both **I** and WARP.

More remarkable is how frequently the mistake has been repeated, though in a slightly different guise, by those who contend that **I** is violated whenever a spoiler tilts an election – as happened in the US presidential elections of 1844, 1848, and 2000. Let x and y be the main candidates, x the more popular, and z the spoiler: z cannot win but draws enough support from x to make y the victor. Then $C(\{x, y\}) = \{x\}$ but $C(\{x, y, z\}) = \{y\}$, again a violation of WARP, or social rationality, not of **I**.

Yes, there is a voting rule that uses Borda scores of a sort and violates **I**, but it is a bizarre rule, not Borda's (although the two are often confused), and no one knows how to implement it. The Borda Rule is based on a separate Borda-score ordering of each subset of A from which a choice is to be made. Instead let $\succ_\mathbf{p}$ be the Borda-score ordering of A itself, the whole universe of alternatives, and $C_\mathbf{p}(\alpha)$ the set of $\succ_\mathbf{p}$-best members of α for any α. Because $\succ$ does not vary with α, C does not represent the Borda Rule. And unlike the Borda Rule, C violates **I**. To see how, let $n = 3$ and $A = \{x, y, z\}$, and compare two profiles:

P	1	2	3	**P′**	1	2	3
2	x	x	y	2	x	x	y
1	y	y	z	1	z	z	x
0	z	z	x	0	y	y	z

Under both profiles, Borda chooses x from $\{x, y\}$. But by the *proposed rule*, $C_\mathbf{P}(\{x, y\}) = \{x, y\}$ and $C_{\mathbf{P}'}(\{x, y\}) = \{x\}$ (i.e., $x \approx_\mathbf{P} y$ and $x \succ_{\mathbf{P}'} y$) although $\mathbf{P}$ and $\mathbf{P}'$ are xy – twins, contrary to $\mathbf{I}$. The problem with implementing the proposed rule is that in practice one does not know how to identify A, the universe of alternatives, much less how voters would preferentially order it: preferential ballots only list members of the prevailing feasible set.

One old view of the restrictive power of $\mathbf{I}$ is quite correct: it bans dependence on interpersonally comparable cardinal utility – on information such as "voter 1 prefers x to y 3.7 times as intensely as 2 prefers y to x." To use such information, we have to represent $\succ$ as a function of *utility profiles* $\mathbf{u} = (u_1, \ldots, u_n)$, $\mathbf{u}' = (u'_1, \ldots, u'_n)$, etc., comprising real-valued "utility" functions on A. The change is merely stylistic if we assume *ordinality*: $\succ_\mathbf{u} = \succ_{\mathbf{u}'}$ whenever each u'_i is an order-preserving transform of u_i ($u'_i(x) > u'_i(y) \leftrightarrow u_i(x) > u_i(y)$ for all x, y). Of course, we have to rewrite $\mathbf{U\mathcal{D}I}$:

$\mathbf{U^u}$ If $u_i(x) > u_i(y)$ for all i, then $x \succ_\mathbf{u} y$.

$\mathbf{\mathcal{D}^u}$ No i is such that, for all x, y, and $\mathbf{u}$, if $u_i(x) > u_i(y)$ but $u_j(x) < u_j(y)$ for every $j \neq i$, then $x \succ_\mathbf{u} y$.

$\mathbf{I^u}$ If $x \succ_\mathbf{u} y$ and if, for every i, u_i and u'_i order $\{x, y\}$ the same way, then $x \succ_{\mathbf{u}'} y$.

But obviously, $\mathbf{I^u}$ implies ordinality. In Sections 4.5 and 4.6, we shall see how to relax $\mathbf{I^u}$ a good deal and still prove an Arrow-style impossibility theorem, indeed one that relaxes $\mathbf{T}$ to the assumption that $\succ_\mathbf{p}$ is always acyclic.

What else does the remarkably controversial $\mathbf{I}$ require? It restricts available information so that C and $\succ$ can reflect voter preferences only between feasible alternatives: $C_\mathbf{p}(\alpha)$ does not depend on preferences between alternatives outside α, nor $\succ_\mathbf{p}$ on preferences between alternatives other than the two being compared. I know of no real or realistic voting rule that violates this requirement, and it would not matter if some did, for as there must be a reasonable way to make social choices in the absence of any given type of information that is not always available.

3.5 PROOF OF ARROW'S THEOREM

In stating and proving Arrow's Theorem and the variations presented in the next two chapters, I shall tacitly assume that $\succ$ is a function from all ordered n-tuples $\mathbf{P}$ of linear orderings of A to asymmetric relations $\succ_{\mathbf{p}}$ on A, with $\succcurlyeq$ and $\approx$ defined as above. When $\mathbf{P}$ is understood from context, I shall drop it and write $\succ$ rather than $\succ_{\mathbf{p}}$. Likewise $\succcurlyeq$ and $\approx$, and even C in later chapters.

Denote subsets of N (*groups* of voters) by g, g', etc., and define:

$xP[g]y$ if and only if $g = \{i \mid xP_i\, y\}$ (the members of g and they alone prefer x to y in $\mathbf{P}$),

and g is *decisive* for (x, y) if and only if $xP[g]y \Rightarrow x \succ_{\mathbf{p}} y$ for all $\mathbf{P}$ (x beats y whenever the members of g and they alone prefer x to y).

Those definitions let us recast U$\cancel{D}$I:

U N is decisive for all pairs (of distinct alternatives).

$\cancel{D}$ No $\{i\}$ is decisive for all pairs.

I   If $x \succ_{\mathbf{p}} y$ and $xP[g]\, y$, then g is decisive for (x, y) (that is, $x \succ_{\mathbf{p}'} y$ *whenever* $xP'[g]y$).

To prove Arrow's Theorem, I shall assume **AU$\cancel{D}$I** and deduce a contradiction, in three steps.

Step I. Some $\{i\}$ is decisive for some pair.

Proof. By **U** and the finitude of N, some g is a smallest decisive set, say for (x, y). Suppose g is empty: $g = \varnothing$. But for some $\mathbf{P}$, $yP[N]x$ and thus $xP[\varnothing]y$, whence $x \succ_{\mathbf{p}} y \succ_{\mathbf{p}} x$ by hypothesis and **U**, contrary to the asymmetry of $\succ_{\mathbf{p}}$. So $g \neq \varnothing$; say $i \in g$.

Now take any third alternative t (by A) and construct $\mathbf{P}$ to fit this picture:

$\{i\}$	$g - \{i\}$	$N - g$
x	t	y
y	x	t
t	y	x

If $t \succ y$, then $g-\{i\}$ is decisive for (t, y) by $\mathbf{I}$ (because $t\ \mathbf{P}[g-\{i\}]y$). But $g-\{i\}$ is too small to be decisive. So $y \succcurlyeq t$. But $x \succ y$ by the decisiveness of g. And thanks to $\mathbf{T}$ we have $x \succ y \succcurlyeq t \Rightarrow x \succ t$. Therefore, $x \succ t$, making $\{i\}$ decisive for (x, t) by $\mathbf{I}$.

Step II. If $\{i\}$ is decisive for any given (x, y) and if t is any third alternative, then $\{i\}$ is also decisive (a) for (x, t) and (b) for (t, y).

Proof. Construct $\mathbf{P}$ as above but erase the middle column. Then for (a) we have $x \succ y$ by hypothesis and $y \succ t$ by $\mathbf{U}$, so $x \succ t$ by $\mathbf{T}$, making $\{i\}$ decisive for (x, t) by $\mathbf{I}$ (because $x\mathbf{P}[\{i\}]t$). For (b), construct $\mathbf{P}$ yet again but with t moved *above* x in the first column, under $\{i\}$. Then $t \succ x$ by $\mathbf{U}$, but $x \succ y$ by hypothesis, so $t \succ y$ by $\mathbf{T}$, making $\{i\}$ decisive for (t, y) by $\mathbf{I}$.

Step III. For all distinct z, w, $\{i\}$ is decisive for (z, w), contrary to $\mathbf{D}$.

Proof. By Step I, $\{i\}$ is decisive for some (x, y). By $\mathbf{A}$, let $t \neq x$, $t \neq z$. Then $\{i\}$ is decisive for (x, t) by Step II (a), hence for (z, t) by Step II (b), hence for (z, w) by Step II (a) again.

Conclusion: **AUDIT** are inconsistent. Equivalently, **AUDI** imply a breakdown of $\mathbf{T}$, Transitivity.

3.6 ON NOT OVERSTATING THE THEOREM

But a breakdown of Transitivity is not necessarily a cycle $(x \succ y \succ z \succ x)$. Instead it might be a case where only social indifference – the tie relation – is nontransitive $(x \approx y \approx z \succ x)$, or one in which social preference (the beat relation) is nontransitive but without being cyclic $(x \succ y \succ z \approx x)$. The interesting intransitivities are cycles, of course: they alone block stability, or best choices, or rationalizability. As you are about to see, however, **AUĐI** do not yield cycles but a modest fortification of **AUĐI** do. I am being emphatic and a bit repetitive because so many scholars have attributed cycles to Arrow or made artful use of sloppy language to obscure the difference between cycles and the less consequential intransitivity found by Arrow. Some distinguished ones have even equated Arrow's Paradox with Condorcet's or said that Arrow proved something about cycles. The law bans robbery, but not every violation of the law is a robbery. **T** bans cycles but not every violation of **T** is a cycle.

Cycles aside, does Arrow's Theorem say anything else of interest? Not much. Why strengthen a ban on cycles to **T** when so many attractive assumptions about $\succ$, albeit stronger ones than **AUĐI**, already imply that even a ban on cycles is too much to assume? Some cite the effect of spoilers as instances of Arrow's Theorem, but as you saw, they violate WARP, and with it social rationality: **AUĐI** have nothing to do with them. Some have said that the theorem reveals the impossibility of an ideal voting rule. To be "ideal," however, a voting rule would have to be far more fair and democratic than required by **AUĐI**. And what is ideal about **T**? Replace "ideal" by "minimally acceptable" and you have a plausible reading of **AUĐI**. But what about **T**? It bans more than cycles, which every realistic voting rule allows. And unlike **U** and **Đ**, its violations are not injustices: they do not hurt anyone. True, Arrow's principal stated subject was not voting rules but social-welfare criteria. He and others have thought that the two subjects are very much alike, but how alike are they? I discuss that question in Section 10.3.

4 Arrovian Cycle Theorems

If we add a bit to **AUⅅI**, we can deduce that $\succ$ flouts not only **T** but
Acyclicity – that $\succ_p$ is sometimes cyclic. In other words, we can turn
Arrow's Theorem into a generalization of the Paradox of Voting. There
are several ways to do that, and one of them allows interpersonal
comparisons of preference intensity.

4.1 FIRST RELAXATION: TRANSITIVE SOCIAL PREFERENCE

As a first step toward getting cycles, or an impossibility theorem
based on the acyclicity of every $\succ_p$ rather than any stronger transitivity condition, let us relax **T** to the transitivity of every $\succ_p$,
or $\succ-$ **Transitivity**. That drops the transitivity of $\approx_p$, making each
$\succ_p$ a partial ordering but not necessarily a weak ordering. This is
important because Sen has long insisted that a social weak ordering is too much to demand but a social partial ordering is reasonable, important too because so many expositors confuse **T** with
$\succ-$ **Transitivity**.

　　Arrow's inconsistency is not preserved: unlike **T**, $\succ-$ **Transitivity**
is consistent with **AUⅅI**. The unanimity rule used by juries
obviously satisfies **AUⅅI** and $\succ-$ **Transitivity**. So it must flout the
assumption that $\approx$, the tie relation, is always transitive. Indeed if
some jurors prefer x to y to z, all the others y to z to x, then z ties x
and x ties y but y beats z ($z \approx x \approx y \succ z$). But of course, the jury rule is
most unusual in mandating ties all over the place.

　　For an interesting impossibility theorem with $\succ-$ **Transitivity** in
place of **T**, we need some restriction on ties, preferably a mild one.
This one will do:

MR If $xP[N-\{i\}]y$, then $x \succ_{\mathbf{p}} y$ or $y \succ_{\mathbf{p}} x$ (if $n-1$ voters share a preference between two alternatives, they cannot tie) (*Minimum Resoluteness*).

Compare this condition with Ward's kindred but much stronger **VU** (Virtual Unanimity), introduced in Section 1.6: if $n-1$ voters prefer x to y, then x beats y. Unlike **MR**, that can block social preferences based on individual rights.

With **T** weakened to $\succ$–**Transitivity** but **MR** added, we can reprove Arrow's Theorem. Only Step I made full use of **T**; Steps II and III relied on $\succ$–**Transitivity**. At Step I, we found $x \succ y \succcurlyeq t$ and inferred $x \succ t$ by **T**. But by **MR**, if *not* $x \succ t$, then $t \succ x$, so $t \succ x \succ y$, whence $t \succ y$ by $\succ$–**Transitivity**, impossible because $y \succcurlyeq t$.

Even a breakdown of $\succ$–**Transitivity** need not be a cycle, however. Unlike $\succ$–**Transitivity**, **Acyclicity** – the general ban on social-preference cycles – is consistent with **AUĐI** plus **MR**. Let $n = 4$, let A have exactly three members, and let $x \succ y$ if and only if three voters prefer x to y. Then **AUĐI** and **MR** are satisfied, and now so is **Acyclicity**. For if three of four voters prefer x to y and three prefer y to z, then it is impossible for three to prefer z to x.

4.2 FROM $\succ$–TRANSITIVITY TO ACYCLICITY, ASSUMING n ALTERNATIVES

One reason **AUĐI** + **MR** are consistent with **Acyclicity** is that **A** lets A have as few as three members when $n > 3$. Instead, assume

A+ A has $n \geq 3$ or more members.

Inconsistency returns.

Proof. In the proof of Arrow's Theorem, we invoked $\succ$–**Transitivity** at Step II (a), where we had $x \succ y \succ t$ and inferred $x \succ t$. Now **Acyclicity** gives us only $x \succcurlyeq t$. But now, too, **MR** implies that $x \succ t$ or $t \succ x$. So $x \succ t$. Step II (b) is similar.

Step I, which shows that some $\{i\}$ is decisive, needs a different approach. In Section 1.6, we saw that, with $n \geq 3$ alternatives, **VU** contradicts **Acyclicity**. So **A+** and **Acyclicity** contradict **VU**: there exist **P**, i, x, and y such that $yP[N–\{i\}]x$ but not $y \succ_\mathbf{p} x$. It follows by **MR** that $x \succ_\mathbf{p} y$, making $\{i\}$ decisive for (x, y) by **I**.

Needless to say, **A+** is rather strong. But as we saw, **AUĐI + MR** by themselves are consistent with **Acyclicity**. Can we relax **A+**?

4.3   WRONG TURN: POSITIVE RESPONSIVENESS

We can, but the best-known way rests on the meretricious tie restriction *Positive Responsiveness*: Whenever x and y are tied, any voter who prefers x can break the tie in y's favor by reversing his preference. After I proved the inconsistency of **A + UĐI** with **MR** and **Acyclicity** (1970), Mas-Colell and Sonnenschein (1972) relaxed **A+** back to **A**, fortified **Đ** a bit – to **D+**, let us say – and proved the inconsistency of **AUĐ + I** with Positive Responsiveness and **Acyclicity**. No progress was made. Obviously, majority rule satisfies Positive Responsiveness, but we need no fancy theorem to tell us that majority rule can spawn cycles. What kills Positive Responsiveness is that it is incompatible with representative democracy and other common institutions.

Positive Responsiveness requires perfect sensitivity to voter preferences. To allow less perfection, I once reproved the theorem after relaxing Positive Responsiveness by changing "any voter" to "any $n/5$ voters," and Duggan has found that "any $n/3$ voters" works too. But even that is incompatible with the election by districts of one of two parties to control a legislature. Witness this case of parties x and y and four districts comprising five voters each:

xxx<u>yy</u>	xxx<u>yy</u>	<u>yy</u>yyy	yyyyy
D_1	D_2	D_3	D_4

Here the parties are tied: D_1 and D_2 support x, D_3 and D_4 y. But if the underlined y votes, 40 percent of the total, are all reversed in favor of x, the tie is not broken. Proportional representation also flouts Positive Responsiveness. Assume a tie between two parties or electoral coalitions: they have won equally many seats. But because there are far fewer seats than votes, a reversal of one or a few votes would rarely break such a tie. Or assume a bi-cameral legislature where x and y are two versions of a bill, both preferred to the status quo by majorities in both chambers. If a large majority of one chamber prefers x to y and the opposite is true in the other chamber, then x ties y in the legislature but no reversal of one or a few votes would change that.

See how unrestrictive Arrow's **AUĐI** are. They are satisfied even by the most odious despotisms: real dictators are far less powerful than those banned by **Đ**. Such modest tie restrictions as **MR** do not contract the **AUĐI** universe very much: it still comprises all democracies and practically every other regime. But Positive Responsiveness shrinks it to practically nothing: all real democracies are gone. It was assumed only because it looked plausible to theorists, myself included, who gave too little thought to what it actually means. As in Section 2.7, I insist that proofs are only as good as their premises.

4.4   THREE OR MORE ALTERNATIVES AND A REASONABLE LIMIT ON TIES: $(2k-2)$-RESOLUTENESS

But for an Arrow-style impossibility theorem involving **Acyclicity** and no strengthening of **A** or **Đ**, we can make a far less restrictive assumption than Positive Responsiveness:

$(2k-2)$**R**   If some tie set has k members, then some decisive set has $2k - 2$ or fewer members $((2k-2)$-*Resoluteness*),

where g is a *tie set* if $x\mathbf{P}[g]\,y$ but $x \approx_{\mathbf{p}} y$ for some **P** and some distinct x, y.

In other words, if k voters ever occupy one side in a tie, then some $2k - 2$ or fewer voters can decide something.

For $k > 2$, this new condition is a sweeping relaxation of Positive Responsiveness: the decisive set need not include or even overlap the original tie set, the alternatives for which it is decisive need not be those that were tied, and unless k is small, the smallest decisive set can be almost twice as big as the given tie set. But for $k \le 2$ the consequences of

(2k – 2)R are a bit more surprising. If $k = 1$, then $2k - 2 = 0$. But no decisive set can have zero members (see proof of Step I, Section 3.5). It follows that no tie set can have but one member. That is, **MR** follows, and we can drop it as a separate assumption. If $k = 2$, then $2k - 2 = 2$. So if some tie set has but two members, then some decisive set must have two too – an odd implication, but one to which I can find no objection.

Still the power of (2k – 2)R means that it must rule out *some* procedures. It does rule out the jury versions of unanimity rule and two-third majority rule – the ones that assume no default alternative. Under them, most votes result in ties. But for that reason, those are very odd rules.

Although **Acyclicity** is consistent with Arrow's **AUÐI**, it *is not consistent with* **AUÐI** + (2k – 2)R.

Proof. Assume **AUÐI, (2k – 2)R**, and **Acyclicity**. Because (2k – 2)R implies **MR**, all we have to redo in our last proof is Step I: some unit is set decisive.

As before, let g be a smallest decisive set, decisive for (x, y), and, as we saw, nonempty. Unless it is already a unit set, partition g into subsets g_1 with k members and g_2 with k or $k - 1$. Again, construct profile **P**, but now a bit differently:

g_1	g_2	$N - (g_1 \cup g_2)$
x	t	y
y	x	t
t	y	x

If $x \succ t$ or $t \succ y$, then g_1 or g_2 is decisive for (x, t) or (t, y) by **I**. But they are too small for that. And if $x \approx t$ or $t \approx y$, then g_1 or g_2 is a tie set, so some decisive set has $2k - 2$ or fewer members. But that is impossible because smallest decisive g has more than $2k - 2$ members. Therefore, $t \succ x$ and $y \succ t$. But $x \succ y$ by the decisiveness of g, contrary to **Acyclicity**. Hence, g must be a unit set after all.

4.5 A SIDE TRIP TO INTERPERSONALLY COMPARABLE CARDINAL UTILITIES

In Section 3.2, we saw that **I** blocks the use of interpersonal comparisons of cardinal utilities, or preference intensities. But in the utility-function framework introduced there, we can relax $\mathbf{I}^u$ considerably to allow social choices to reflect such comparisons and still reprove the cycle theorem of Section 4.2, the one based on **MR** and **A+**. Obviously, **MR** and **Acyclicity** have to be recast in the manner of $\mathbf{U}^u$, $\mathcal{D}^u$, and $\mathbf{I}^u$:

MR^u   If $u_i(x) > u_i(y)$ but $u_j(y) > u_j(x)$ for every $j \neq i$, then $x \succ_\mathbf{u}$ y or $y \succ_\mathbf{u} x$.

Acyclicity^u   Never $x_1 \succ_\mathbf{u} x_2 \succ_\mathbf{u} \cdots \succ_\mathbf{u} x_k \succ_\mathbf{u} x_1$.

      What about that relaxation of $\mathbf{I}^u$? Suppose $x \succ_\mathbf{u} y$ and individual preferences between x and y (but not necessarily their cardinal utilities) are the same in $\mathbf{u}'$ as in $\mathbf{u}$. Then $\mathbf{I}^u$ says that $x \succ_{\mathbf{u}'} y$. My weaker condition also says that $x \succ_{\mathbf{u}'} y$, but not always. It says so only in the special case where, according to $\mathbf{u}$, just one voter, i, prefers x to y, all others prefer y to x, y has both an *aggregate utility* and a *minimum utility* greater than or equal to x's, and y's *distribution* of utility to voters other than i is the same as x's (hence equally fair or unfair) except for a uniform increase (hence uncontroversially superior). In such an unlikely case, the fact that x beats y under $\mathbf{u}$ must be based on some special right or power or authority of i's, not on cardinal utilities. So it is reasonable to expect that x would beat y under ordinally similar $\mathbf{u}'$ as well. In short:

MI   Suppose $u_i(x) > u_i(y)$ but $u_j(y) > u_j(x)$ for all $j \neq i$,
$u'_i(x) > u'_i(y)$ but $u'_j(y) > u'_j(x)$ for all $j \neq i$,

$$\sum_{j=1}^n u_j(y) \geq \sum_{j=1}^n u_j(x),$$

$u_i(y) \geq u_j(x)$ for some j,
and   for some d, $u_j(y) - u_j(x) = d$ for all $j \neq i$.
Then if $x \succ_\mathbf{u} y$, $x \succ_{\mathbf{u}'} y$ (*Minimum Independence*).

One might object to **MR^u** that it bans ties when one voter prefers x to y, all others y to x, and x and y have the same aggregate utility. Should x and y not tie in such a case? The answer is threefold: (1) A mere tie would be utterly unrealistic when all but one voter share a preference. (2) Even if interpersonal comparisons were possible, they would doubtless be somewhat error-prone and imprecise. (3) The "greatest good" ought to be combined with the "greatest number," if not always, then at least to avoid a mere coin toss, especially when the "greatest number" is $n - 1$ – although **MR^u** allows $x \succ y$ in that case. Actually, a close reading of the proof below shows that we could have relaxed **MR^u** as follows:

If **u** satisfies the hypothesis of **MI**, then $x \succ_u y$ or $y \succ_u x$.

But **MR^u** is already so reasonable that I see no gain from the added complexity.

4.6 PROOF OF INCONSISTENCY

First, let us recast **MI** in a style closer to earlier formulations. Define:

$x\mathbf{u}[g]y$ if and only if $u_i(x) > u_i(y)$ for all i in g whereas $u_i(y) > u_i(x)$ for all i in N–g,

and g is *decisive^u* for (x, y) if and only if $x\mathbf{u}[g]y \Rightarrow x \succ_u y$ for all **u**.

Then **MI** says:

Suppose

$$x\mathbf{u}[\{i\}]y,$$

$$\sum_{j=1}^{n} u_j(y) \geq \sum_{j=1}^{n} u_j(x),$$

$u_i(y) \geq u_j(x)$ for some j,

and   for some d, $u_j(y) - u_j(x) = d$ for all $j \neq i$.

Then $x \succ_u y \Rightarrow \{i\}$ is decisive^u for (x, y).

To prove that $\mathbf{A+}$, $\mathbf{U^u}$, $\mathbf{D^u}$, $\mathbf{MR^u}$, $\mathbf{Acyclicity^u}$, and $\mathbf{MI}$ are inconsistent, go back to the original proof in Section 4.2. It invoked three profiles of preference orderings, but we can turn them into utility profiles. At Step I, we used our old friend the $n \times n$ profile of Section 1.6. Here it is again, but with utility numbers added:

utility	1	2	3	...	i	...	n
n	x_1	x_2	x_3		x_i		x_n
$n-1$	x_2	x_3	x_4		x_{i+1}		x_1
$n-2$	x_3	x_4	.		.		x_2
.	.	.	.		.		x_3
.	.	.	.		x_n		.
.	.	.	.		x_1		.
3	.	.	$x_n.$		.		.
2	.	x_n	x_1		.		.
1	x_n	x_1	x_2		x_{i-1}		x_{n-1}

We found that $x_i \succ x_{i-1}$ for some i, or maybe $x_1 \succ x_n$. Say $x_3 \succ x_2$. Because voter 3 alone prefers x_3 to x_2, $\mathbf{I}$ lets us infer that $\{3\}$ is decisive for (x_3, x_2). Now $\mathbf{MI}$ does too because the perfect symmetry of the profile ensures that any two alternatives, including x_2 and x_3, have the same aggregate utility $((n^2 + n)/2)$ and the same minimum (1), and because the x_2 and x_3 utility distributions to $N - \{3\}$ are $(n - 1, n, 2, \ldots, n - 2)$ and $(n - 2, n - 1, 1, \ldots, n - 3)$.

Step II (a) and (b) invoked two profiles, to which I shall now add utilities:

Utility	$\{i\}$	$N - \{i\}$	$\{i\}$	$N - \{i\}$
3	x	y	t	
2	y	t	x	y
1	t	x	y	t
0				x

In the first, we found that $x \succ t$ and concluded, by $\mathbf{I}$, that $\{i\}$ is decisive for (x, t). $\mathbf{MI}$ implies the same because i alone prefers x to t, because t has an aggregate utility $(2n - 1)$ greater than x's $(n - 2)$ and the same minimum utility (1), and because their respective distributions to $N - \{i\}$ are $(2, 2, \ldots, 2)$ and $(1, 1, \ldots, 1)$. In the second profile, we found that $t \succ y$ and used **I** to infer that $\{i\}$ is decisive for (t, y). With **MI** we can do the same because i alone prefers t to y, because y has an aggregate utility $(2n - 1)$ greater than t's $(n - 2)$ and the same minimum utility (1), and because their respective distributions to $N - \{i\}$ are $(2, 2, \ldots,)$ and $(1, 1, \ldots, 1)$.

5   Second Line of Cycle Theorems: Condorcet Generalizations

These theorems take off from Condorcet, who discovered cycles, rather than Arrow, who had nothing to say about cycles. They directly generalize the Paradox of Voting, in proof as well as content. The most general of them states a sufficient condition for cycles that is demonstrably as general as possible, necessary as well as sufficient.

5.1   SIMPLE LATIN-SQUARE CONSTRUCTIONS: THE THEOREMS OF WARD, BROWN, AND NAKAMURA

Look again at the Paradox of Voting:

1	2	3
x	y	z
y	z	x
z	x	y

Then look again at the $n \times n$ profile used to prove Ward's Theorem in Section 1.6, to derive a cycle from **VU** (*Virtual Unanimity:* $n - 1$ voters prefer x to $y \Rightarrow x \succ y$). It is displayed again in Section 4.6. The big profile generalizes the smaller one. Both are *latin squares*: their columns from left to right are the same as are their rows from top to bottom.

Ward's discovery was rediscovered in effect by Brown (1975), but I do not think he realized it. Call g *universally decisive* if it is decisive for every pair of alternatives. Brown assumed there is no "collegium," no nonempty subset of all universally decisive sets. More simply: no voter belongs to all universally decisive sets. So for every i, some universally decisive set excludes i. Now assume:

M   If g is decisive for (x, y) and $g \subseteq h$, then h is decisive for (x, y)
         (*Monotonicity*).

Since $N - \{i\}$ is a superset of any universally decisive set that excludes i, it follows by **M** that $N - \{i\}$ is universally decisive too. But that is just **VU**. Like Ward, Brown combines that condition with **A+** to get a cycle.

To see all this in a slightly different light, define:

g is *impotent* for (x, y) if and only if $N - g$ is decisive for (y, x).

Under majority rule, minorities are universally impotent, impotent for every pair of alternatives. **VU** says that all unit sets of voters are. Here is a more general assumption:

N   For some $m \le n$, there exists a partition of N into m univer-
         sally impotent subsets.

In case $m < n$ (as is often true), we can use an $m \times m$ latin square, comprising fewer than n alternatives, to derive a cycle: each column is the preference ordering of one universally impotent set. That is exactly what we did with Condorcet's 3×3 latin square in Section 1.2, where we assumed majority rule and interpreted 1, 2, and 3 as three minorities. Similarly, if N can be partitioned into five universally impotent sets $g_1, \ldots, g_5$, we can construct the 5×5 latin-square profile:

g_1	g_2	g_3	g_4	g_5
x_1	x_2	x_3	x_4	x_5
x_2	x_3	x_4	x_5	x_1
x_3	x_4	x_5	x_1	x_2
x_4	x_5	x_1	x_2	x_3
x_5	x_1	x_2	x_3	x_4

Because g_1 is universally impotent, the union of $g_2, \ldots, g_5$ is universally decisive. And because its members all prefer x_5 to x_1, $x_5 \succ x_1$. Likewise, $x_1 \succ x_2 \succ x_3 \succ x_4 \succ x_5$.

Assumption **N** is tantamount to Nakamura's (1979). He assumed that some $m \le n$ universally decisive sets, say $d_1, \ldots, d_m$, have no member in common. If so, there exists a partition of N into universally impotent subsets $g_1, \ldots, g_m$, to wit:

$$g_1 = N - d_1$$
$$g_{i+1} = d_1 \cap \cdots \cap d_i - d_{i+1}.$$

Proof. Because each d_i is universally decisive, each $N - d_i$ is universally impotent, making each $g_i \subseteq N - d_i$ universally impotent too, thanks to **M**. And by construction, $g_1, \ldots, g_m$ are mutually disjoint. They also exhaust N: each i belongs to one of them, else i would belong to every d_j, contrary to hypothesis. In case some g_i ends up empty, we can delete it from the list, making m even smaller. To prove the converse, partition N into universally impotent $g_1, \ldots, g_m$. That makes $N - g_1, \ldots, N - g_m$ universally decisive. Had they a member in common, it could not belong to any g_i, so $\{g_1, \ldots, g_m\}$ would not be a partition of N after all.

5.2 A GENERAL CONDITION FOR CYCLES

For a cycle, we do not need *universal* decisiveness or impotence. It is enough that N have a partition into two or more subsets, $g_1, \ldots, g_m$, each impotent for *some* pair of alternatives, say g_i for (x_i, y_i), with distinct names of distinct objects. The latter ensures that the sets $X = \{x_1, \ldots, x_m\}$, $Y = \{y_1, \ldots, y_m\}$, and $G = \{g_1, \ldots, g_m\}$ have m members each and share none of them. But we can relax that to let X and Y overlap, within limits: never $x_i = y_i$ of course, and more generally, no proper subset of X is the same as any *identically indexed* subset of Y (e.g. $\{x_1, x_4\} \neq \{y_1, y_4\}$), but possibly $X = Y$. In short:

(*)   For some $m \geq 2$, there exist an m-member partition
                        $G = \{g_1, \ldots, g_m\}$ of N and m-member sets $X = \{x_1, \ldots,$
                        $x_m\}$ and $Y = \{y_1, \ldots, y_m\}$ such that

                            never $\{x_i \mid i \in S\} = \{y_i \mid i \in S\}$ if $\varnothing \neq S \subset N$
                        and   each g_i is impotent for $\{x_i, y_i\}$.

Later I shall relax and relabel (*).

Assuming **M**, (*) has a noteworthy equivalent:

                        For some $m \geq 2$, there are subsets $d_1, \ldots, d_m$ of N with no
                        member in common and m – member sets $\{x_1, \ldots, x_m\}$
                        and $\{y_1, \ldots, y_m\}$ such that

                            never $\{x_i \mid i \in S\} = \{y_i \mid i \in S\}$ if $\varnothing \neq S \subset N$
                        and   each d_i is decisive for $\{y_i, x_i\}$.

Equivalence is proved in much the same way as that of **N** to
Nakamura's assumption.

To deduce that $\succ_\mathbf{p}$ is sometimes cyclic, I shall assume little
more than (*): just (*) and **U**.

5.3   PROOF THAT CYCLES ARE ALLOWED

Let m, G, X, and Y be as in (*). Call i *synonymous* with j if $x_i = y_j$.
Because never $x_i = y_i$, no i is synonymous with itself. But because the
xs and ys are both m in number, each i is synonymous with at most
one j. And because subscript indices are arbitrary, if the synonymy
relation is cyclic, we may assume that 1 is synonymous with 2,
which is synonymous with 3, ..., which is synonymous with k,
which is synonymous with 1, for some $k \leq m$. Then $x_1 = y_2$, $x_2 =$
$y_3, \ldots, x_{k-1} = y_k$, and $x_k = y_1$. It follows that $\{x_1, \ldots, x_k\} = \{y_1, \ldots, y_k\}$.
But that contradicts (*) unless $k = m$. On the other hand, if the
relation is *not* cyclic, we may assume that each $i < m$ is synonymous
at most with $i + 1$ and m is synonymous with nothing. Either way,
each x_i other than x_m is equal to no y but at most y_{i+1}, and x_m is equal
at most to y_1.

That lets us construct profile **P**:

g_1	g_2	$\cdots$	g_i	$\cdots$	g_m
x_1	x_2		x_i		x_m
(y_2)	(y_3)		(y_{i+1})		(y_1)
x_2	.		x_{i+1}		x_1
(y_3)	.		(y_{i+2})		(y_2)
.	.		.		.
.	x_{i-1}		.		.
.	(y_i)		.		.
x_{i-1}	x_i		x_m		x_{i-1}
(y_i)	(y_{i+1})		(y_1)		(y_i)
x_i	.		x_1		x_i
(y_{i+1})	.		(y_2)		(y_{i+1})
.	.		.		.
.	x_m		.		.
.	(y_1)		.		.
x_m	x_1		x_{i-1}		x_{m-1}
(y_1)	(y_2)		(y_i)		(y_m)

Here, an x followed by a parenthetical y means that x is just above y unless $x = y$. Note that x_i is always above y_{i+1} (x_i P_j y_{i+1} for all j), ensuring $x_i \succ y_{i+1}$ by **U**, unless $x_i = y_{i+1}$. Likewise x_m and y_1. But each g_i is impotent for (x_i, y_i), and every other g_j has y_i above x_i, ensuring $y_i \succ x_i$. Hence the cycle:

$$x_1(\succ y_2)\succ x_2(\succ y_3)\cdots\succ x_i(\succ y_{1+1})\cdots\succ x_m(\succ y_1)\succ x_1,$$

where the parenthetical part of each "$x (\succ y)$" is to be read if $x \neq y$ but ignored if $x = y$.

5.4   HOW EARLIER RESULTS AND PROOFS FIT THE PATTERN

Assumption (*) directly generalizes the assumptions of Condorcet, Ward, Brown, and Nakamura, chiefly by replacing universal impotence (or decisiveness) with impotence for *a pair* – and not assuming much about connections between pairs. Their proofs are generalized too: **P** is a *generalized latin square*, one which *may* have more alternatives (and rows) than columns, if that is needed to form unanimous preferences that fill gaps in a cyclic chain of social preferences. For example, if $m = 3$ and X and Y share no members, then **P** is

g_1	g_2	g_3
x_1	x_2	x_3
y_2	y_3	y_1
x_2	x_3	x_1
y_3	y_1	y_2
x_3	x_1	x_2
y_1	y_2	y_3

Because each g_i is impotent for (x_i, y_i), we have $y_1 \succ x_1$, $y_2 \succ x_2$, and $y_3 \succ x_3$. But because x_1 is unanimously preferred to y_2, x_2 to y_3, and x_3 to y_1, we also have $x_1 \succ y_2$, $x_2 \succ y_3$, and $x_3 \succ y_1$, completing a cycle. In the proof, the re-indexing of alternatives and the use of parentheses allowed any degree of overlap between X and Y.

It is less obvious but nonetheless true that my theorem generalizes Sen's Liberal Paradox (from Section 1.7). His most general version assumes:

(L***)   There exist i, j, x, y, z, w such that $\{i\}$ is decisive for (x, y), $\{j\}$ is decisive for (z, w), and these distinctions hold: $i \neq j$, $x \neq y$, $z \neq w$, $x \neq z$, and $y \neq w$.

It follows by **M** (which Sen also assumes) that we can partition N into two decisive subsets, say g (containing i) for (x, y) and h (containing j) for (z, w). That makes h impotent for (y, x) and g for (w, z) – an instance of (*). Now construct:

g	h
w	y
(x)	(z)
y	w
(z)	(x)

This is a generalized latin square, with parentheses interpreted as in Section 5.3. By **U**, we have $w \succ x$ unless $w = x$, and $y \succ z$ unless $y = z$. But we also have $x \succ y$ and $z \succ w$. In short, $w (\succ x) \succ y (\succ z) \succ w$.

The three Arrovian cycle theorems of Chapter 3 rest on assumptions that do not resemble (*), but they implicitly assume (*), as you will see in Section 5.6, and in each case the two main steps of proof used generalized latin squares. For the first and third theorems (based on **AUDI** plus **MR** and $\mathbf{A + U^U D^U}$ **MI** plus **MR^U**), Step I used a plain $n \times n$ latin square. For the second (based on **AUDI** plus $(2k-2)$**R**), Step I instead used the first of these three profiles:

g_1	g_2	$N-(g_1 \cup g_2)$	$\{i\}$	$N-\{t\}$	$\{i\}$	$N-\{i\}$
x	t	y	x	y	t	y
y	x	t	y	t	x	t
t	y	x	t	x	y	x

Switch the second and third columns and you have a 3×3 latin square. For all three theorems, Step II used the remaining two profiles. Each is a generalized latin square, obtainable from a plain 2×2 latin square by adding a unanimous preference for y to t in the one case, t to x in the other.

Why latin squares to begin with? Set aside the need for gap-filling unanimous preferences by assuming $X = Y$. Thanks to the re-indexing of alternatives, we may further assume that each $g_{i>1}$ is impotent for (x_i, x_{i-1}), and g_1 for (x_1, x_m). To turn these power relationships into a cycle, we must construct a profile that has $x_{i>1}$ above x_{i-1} in the ith column, and x_1 above x_m in the first, while reversing those orders in every other column. The result is automatically an $m \times m$ latin square, with $x_1 \succ x_2 \succ \cdots \succ x_m \succ x_1$.

5.5 INDIVIDUAL INDIFFERENCE AND THE MOST GENERAL CYCLE-SUFFICIENCY CONDITION OF ALL

So far I have been assuming that $\succ$ is defined only for profiles of *linear* orderings of A, weak orderings devoid of indifferences between distinct alternatives. But to have the most general possible condition for cycles, we must allow voter indifference, opening the domain of $\succ$ to *all profiles of weak orderings of A*. If we do, then (*) is too strong, not general enough, not *necessary* for a cycle. A dictatorship that lets majorities rule when the dictator is indifferent can create cycles but does not satisfy (*): in no partition of N is the dictator's subset impotent.

But for dictator i, we can partition $N–\{i\}$ into subsets that are "impotent *relative* to $\{i\}$," impotent when i is indifferent. So define:

> g is *impotent relative to h* for (x, y) if and only if g and h are disjoint and $y \succ_p x$ for every **P** in which $xP[g]y$ and $yP[N –(g{\cup}h)]x$ (y beats x in every profile in which the voters in g prefer x to y and those *not* in g or h prefer y to x, so those in h – which may be empty – are indifferent).

The promised relaxation of (*) adds a set g, possibly empty, to the partition of N and relativizes impotence to g:

IP   For some $m \geq 2$, there exist an $(m + 1)$ – member partition $G = \{g, g_1, \ldots, g_m\}$ of N and m – member sets $X =\{x_1, \ldots, x_m\}$ and $Y =\{y_1, \ldots, y_m\}$ such that
never $\{x_i \mid i \in S\} = \{y_i \mid i \in S\}$ if $\emptyset \neq S \subset N$,
and each g_i is impotent relative to g for (x_i, y_i) (*Impotence Partition*).

Like impotence, decisiveness can be relativized to a set of indifferent voters: just replace $y \succ x$ by $x \succ y$ in the definition. And like **N** and (*), **IP** has a decisive-set equivalent: in the formulation of Section 5.2, just add d to the list $d_1, \ldots, d_m$ and relativize the decisiveness of each d_i to d.

With (*) thus relaxed, we must strengthen **U** a bit to accommodate voter indifference:

U+   If $xP_i y$ for some i but $yP_i x$ for no i, then $x \succ y$.

The proof is exactly the same as in Section 5.3 except that we must add a column to **P**, headed by g, representing a (strict) weak ordering that is empty, in effect a preference ordering that ranks all the members of $X \cup Y$ at the same level, and in the text we must relativize impotence to g.

5.6   THE NECESSITY THEOREM

The point of relaxing (*) to **IP** is to prove that **IP** is as general as possible: given a couple of background assumptions, **IP** is not only sufficient but *necessary* for a social-preference cycle under some profile. One background assumption is merely that, for some cycle, not all voters are indifferent between every pair of alternatives in the cycle. The other combines **M** with **I**, Monotonicity with the Independence of Irrelevant Alternatives:

MI   Suppose **P** and **P'** are so related that $xP_i y \Rightarrow xP'_i y$ and $yP'_i x \Rightarrow yP_i x$ for all i. Then $x \succ_\mathbf{p} y \Rightarrow x \succ_{\mathbf{p'}} y$ (*Monotone Independence*).

To prove the necessity theorem, we shall need a bit more notation (to handle voter indifference) and a lemma. Define R_i and I_i in terms of P_i as in Section 3.1.

Lemma. Assume **MI**. Suppose $x \succ_\mathbf{p} y$, $g \subseteq \{i \mid yP_i x\}$, and $h \subseteq \{i \mid xI_i y\}$. Then g is impotent relative to h for (y, x).

Proof. Obviously, g and h are disjoint, so it suffices take any **P'** in which $g = \{i \mid y P'_i x\}$ and $N-(g \cup h) = \{i \mid x P'_i y\}$ and show that $x \succ_{\mathbf{p'}} y$. But if $x P_i y$, then $i \neq g$ and $i \neq h$ by hypothesis of the lemma, so $i \in N-(g \cup h)$, that is, $xP'_i y$. And if $yP'_i x$, then $i \in g$, whence $yP_i x$. But $x \succ_\mathbf{p} y$. Therefore, $x \succ_{\mathbf{p'}} y$ by **MI**.

To prove the necessity theorem, assume **MI** and suppose $xP_j y$ for some j and some x, y in some $\succ_\mathbf{p}$-cycle. I shall deduce that $\succ$ satisfies **IP**.

Obviously, every $\succ_\mathbf{p}$-cycle is a union of one or more *minimum subcycles*, subcycles that include no smaller ones. By hypothesis, there exist j, x, y, and a cycle K such that $xP_j y$ and $x, y \in K$. But suppose that $tI_i u$ for all t, u in every minimum subcycle of K. Then x and y must belong to different minimum subcycles, but as subcycles of K

the latter must belong to a chain of overlapping minimum subcycles. It follows that $x = z_1 \, I_j \, z_2 \, I_j \cdots I_j \, z_k = y$ for some $z_1, \ldots, z_k$ in K. But then, by the transitivity properties of weak orderings, $x I_j \, y$, contrary to hypothesis. Hence, there exists a minimum subcycle $\{z_1, \ldots, z_m\}$ of K such that

$$\text{not } z_1 \, I_j \, z_2 \, I_j \cdots I_j \, z_m \text{ for some } j. \tag{I}$$

Because $\{z_1, \ldots, z_m\}$ is a minimum cycle, we may suppose that $z_1 \succ_p z_2 \succ_p \cdots z_m \succ_p z_{m+1} = z_1$ and the sequences $(z_1, \ldots, z_m)$ and $(z_2, \ldots, z_{m+1})$ have no repetitions. And because $\succ_p$ is asymmetric, $m \geq 2$.

Now define $g, g_1, \ldots, g_m$ as follows:

$$g = \{j | z_1 \, I_j \, z_2 \, I_j \cdots z_m \, I_j \, z_{m+1}\},$$
$$g_1 = \{j | z_2 \, P_j \, z_1\},$$
$$g_{i+1} = \{j | z_{i+2} \, P_j \, z_{i+1}\} - (g_1 \cup \cdots \cup g_i).$$

Then $g \subseteq \{j \mid z_{i+1} \, I_j \, z_i\}$ and $g_i \subseteq \{j \mid z_{i+1} \, P_j \, z_i\}$ for every $i \leq m$. So by the lemma, each g_i is impotent relative to g for (z_{i+1}, z_i).

Because the definitions of $g, g_1, \ldots, g_m$ obviously ensure pairwise disjointness, to show that $\{g, g_1, \ldots, g_m\}$ is a partition of N it suffices to show that every j belongs to some g_i or to g. Suppose j belongs to no g_i. Then *not* $z_{i+1} \, P_j \, z_i$, $i = 1, 2, \ldots, m$. That is, $z_1 \, R_j \, z_2 \, R_j \cdots R_j \, z_{m+1} = z_1$. It follows by the transitivity properties of weak orderings that $z_1 \, R_j \, z_i \, R_j \, z_1$ for all i, whence $z_1 \, I_j \, z_2 \, I_j \cdots I_j \, z_m$. Therefore, $j \in g$.

Now let $(x_1, \ldots, x_m) = (z_2, \ldots, z_{m+1})$ and $(y_1, \ldots, y_m) = (z_1, \ldots, z_m)$, so that each g_i is impotent relative to g for (x_i, y_i). Because those two z-sequences have no repetitions, never $x_i = x_j$ or $y_i = y_j$ if $i \neq j$. And because of how the x- and y-indices are staggered between the two sequences, never $\{x_i \mid i \in S\} = \{y_i \mid i \in S\}$ if $\varnothing \neq S \subset \{1, \ldots, m\}$.

In case $\varnothing$ occurs more than once in the sequence $(g_1, \ldots, g_m)$, delete all occurrences but the first, along with the corresponding pairs from the sequence $((x_1, y_1), \ldots, (x_m, y_m))$. Let $(g'_1, \ldots, g'_{m'})$ and $((x'_1, y'_1), \ldots, (x'_{m'}, y'_{m'}))$ be the resulting sequences. Obviously, $\{g, g'_i, \ldots, g'_{m'}\}$ is still a partition of N, with each g'_i impotent relative to g for (x'_i, y'_i). Because such deletions cannot undo distinctions within or between the sets $\{x_1, \ldots, x_m\}$ and $\{y_1, \ldots, y_m\}$, we have: never $x'_i = x'_j$ or $y'_i = y'_j$ if $i \neq j$, and never $\{x'_i \mid i \in S\} = \{y'_i \mid y \in S\}$ if $\emptyset \neq S \subset \{1, 2, \ldots, m'\}$. But now, if $i \neq j$, then g'_i and g'_j cannot both be empty, and, thus, because distinct g'_i and g'_j are disjoint by definition: never $g'_i = g'_j$ if $i \neq j$.

To complete the derivation of **IP**, we must show that $m' \geq 2$. Suppose not: $m' = 1$. But $m \geq 2$, and $(g'_1, \ldots, g'_{m'}) = (g_1)$ was obtained by deleting all but the first occurrence of $\emptyset$ from $(g_1, \ldots, g_m)$. It follows that g_1 is the first occurrence of $\emptyset$ and $g_1, \ldots, g_m$ are all empty, whence $N = g$, so $z_1 \ I_j \ z_2 \ I_j \cdots I_j \ z_m$ for all j, contrary to (**I**).

6 Top Cycles in a Fixed Feasible Set

Following Arrow and the classical framework of rational choice, we have allowed the set of feasible alternatives to vary, and in one way that has weakened results: a cycle blocks any stable or unbeaten choice from *some* subset of A, some potential feasible set, but not necessarily from *any given* set. However, we can reframe those results so that A is no longer the universe of alternatives but instead comprises the feasible alternatives on any given occasion. Besides strengthening old results in one way, that will give us a more flexible framework in which to discuss the strategic consequences of cycles in the next chapter.

6.1 NEW BOTTLE, OLD WINES

But if A is a fixed feasible set, we can no longer let the feasible set vary. How, then, can we frame classical rationality, a condition on $C_\mathbf{p}$ and $\succ_\mathbf{p}$? And if we cannot, then what is the significance of social-preference cycles? And what is social preference itself if not pairwise social choice, social choice from two-member subsets of A?

Answer: Even a small subset α of A, possibly a pair set, becomes *in effect* the feasible set when everyone prefers every alternative in α to every alternative outside α. At least in that case, the social choice from A has to come from α and alternatives outside α may be ignored. At least in that case, voter preferences have *reduced* the feasible set from A to α – or so may we reasonably assume.

To formalize this idea, let function Γ turn every profile $\mathbf{P}$ of linear orderings of A into a nonempty subset $\Gamma_\mathbf{p}$ of A, the choice set from A under $\mathbf{P}$. In other words, assuming finite A, let $\Gamma_\mathbf{p} = C_\mathbf{p}(A)$ in the language of Section 3.1. Next define:

A *top set* in **P** is any α such that $xP_i y$ for every i, every x in α, and every y in A–α,

where α, β, etc, still denote finite, nonempty subsets of A. Now assume:

TS   If α is a top set in **P**, then $\Gamma_\mathbf{p} \subseteq \alpha$ (*Top Set Condition*).

That lets us define our old social-choice function C, which depends on a variable feasible set:

$$C_\mathbf{p}(\alpha) \;=\; \Gamma_{\mathbf{p}^\alpha}$$

where $\mathbf{P}^\alpha$ = the result of moving the members of α to the top of every ordering in **P**, leaving all else the same (so preferences within α and within $A - \alpha$ do not change).

Since Chapter 3, $C(\alpha)$ has comprised the alternatives that could be chosen (their choice would be permissible) if α were the feasible set. Now it comprises the alternatives that could be chosen if α were *in effect* the feasible set – if α occupied top position, that is. With C in hand we can define social preference as before:

$x \succ_\mathbf{p} y$ if and only if $x \neq y$ and $C_\mathbf{p}(\{x, y\}) = \{x\}$. (i.e., if and only if $x \neq y$ and $\Gamma_\mathbf{p}\{x, y\} = \{x\}$).

The assumptions about A, n, and $\succ$ in Chapters 4 and 5 are as plausible as ever. But our new framework lets us strengthen the results proved there.

6.2   TOP CYCLES

Acyclicity bans cycles, and with them finite, nonempty subsets of A that lack stable members. A weaker assumption bans only top cycles, where:

A *top cycle* in **P** is any $\succ_\mathbf{p}$ – cycle γ (any $\gamma = \{x_1, \ldots, x_k\}$ with $x_1 \succ_\mathbf{p} x_2 \succ_\mathbf{p} \cdots \succ_\mathbf{p} x_k \succ_\mathbf{p} x_1$) such that $x \succ_\mathbf{p} y$ for every x in γ and y in $A - \gamma$.

That blocks stable or unbeaten choices from A itself, our fixed feasible set. A top cycle need not be a top set: every member beats every nonmember, but maybe not unanimously. Thanks to **U**, however, any cycle that is also a top set in **P** is a top cycle in **P**; I shall call it a *top-set cycle*.

In Section 4.4, we proved that **AUĐI**, $(2k - 2)$**R**, and **Acyclicity** are inconsistent. There we doubly recycled steps I, IIa, and IIb from the proof of Arrow's Theorem (Sections 3.5), and at each step constructed **P** to make $\succ_p$ cyclic (or cyclic unless $\{i\}$ is decisive for a certain pair of alternatives). Having said nothing about the alternatives outside the cycle, we may assume that **P** is constructed so all of them are ranked below every cycle member in $P_1, \ldots, P_n$. That makes the cycle a top set, hence a top cycle: all its members are unanimously preferred to everything else.

So **AUĐI** + $(2k- 2)$**R** are inconsistent, not only with **Acyclicity**, the general ban on cycles, but with a ban on top cycles, indeed top-set cycles. In other words, **AUĐI** + $(2k- 2)$**R** *imply the existence of a top-set cycle under some* **P**. Obviously, that blocks any stable choice from A.

In the proofs of Sections 4.2 and 4.6, the cycle formed at Step I is larger in most cases: based on an $n \times n$ latin-square profile, it comprises n alternatives. But we can still construct **P** so that every voter ranks each member of the cycle above everything else, again making it a top-set cycle. So **A** + **UĐI** + **MR** *imply the existence of a top-set cycle under some* **P**, and likewise **A**+, $\mathbf{U^u}$, $\mathbf{Đ^u}$, $\mathbf{MR^u}$, and **MI** under some utility profile **u**. And in the proofs of Sections 5.3 and 5.4, we can place every alternative not in the cycle below every cycle alternative in each voter's preference ordering, ensuring that $(^\star)$ + **U**, or **IP** + **U**+, also imply the existence of a top-set cycle under some **P**.

What I have said about cycles can be said about other intransitivities. A violation of **T** or $\succ$–**Transitivity** has the form $x \succ_p y \succcurlyeq_p z \succcurlyeq_p x$ or $_p x \succ_p y \succ_p z \succcurlyeq_p x$, and in each case we can construct **P** so $\{x, y, z\}$ is a top set. Hence, **AUĐI** and **AUĐI** + **MR** imply the existence of a top-set violation of **T** or $\succ$–**Transitivity**, a top set $\{x, y, z\}$ with $x \succ_p y \succeq_p$ $z \succeq_p x$ or $x \succ_p y \succ_p z \succeq_p x$ under some **P**.

6.3   TRICYCLES AND ALL-INCLUSIVE TIGHT CYCLES

We can show more. In these doubly recycled Steps I, IIa, and IIb, the cycle constructed as each step consists of three alternatives, e.g. x, y, t. So **AUÐI** + $(2k-2)$**R** are inconsistent with a ban on top-set *tricycles*. Those conditions *imply the existence of a three-member top-set cycle under some* **P**.

We can show even more. Instead of a ban on top-set tricycles, we can replace **Acyclicity** with a ban on *all-inclusive tight cycles*. An all-inclusive cycle exhausts A, of course. In a tight cycle, every member (x) beats or is beaten by every other member (y), which it beats if not directly $(x \succ y)$ then at one or two removes $(x \succ z \succ y$ or $x \succ z \succ w \succ y$ for some $z, w)$. At Steps I and II, replace t in **P** by some linear ordering ρ of $A - \{x, y\}$. At Step I, we inferred from **AUÐI** + $(2k-2)$**R** that $x \succ_p y \succ_p$ $t \succ_p x$ unless $g = \{i\}$. Now we have $x \succ_p y \succ_p u \succ_p x$ for every u in $A - \{x, y\}$ – an all-inclusive tight cycle – unless $g = \{i\}$. At Step IIa, we inferred $x \succ_p$ $y \succ_p t \succ_p x$ unless $\{i\}$ is decisive for (x, t). If, in our new **P**, we construct ρ so t is at the bottom $(u \rho t$ for every u in $A - \{x, y, t\})$, we now have (1) $x \succ_p$ $y \succ_p u$ for every u in $A - \{x, y\}$, (2) $u \succ_p v$ whenever $u \rho v$ by **U**, and (3) $t \succ_p$ x – again an all-inclusive tight cycle – unless $\{i\}$ is decisive for (x, t). Step IIb is similar except that ρ is moved above x in the first column (voter i's preference ordering) and t is moved to the top of ρ. To sum up: **AUÐI** + $(2k-2)$**R** *imply the existence of an all-inclusive tight cycle under some* **P**.

A top cycle of any sort, large or small, tight or loose, rules out best or stable alternatives to prescribe or predict. But that may not be so bad. For in an obvious sense, a top cycle is a best or stable *set*, itself a plausible thing to prescribe or predict, and an attractive one too if it is small. But not if it is all-inclusive. I do not mean that small cycles are uninteresting. In Sections 7.1 and 7.2, we shall find that in strategic contexts it is top tricycles that are especially consequential.

Suppose a member x of a top cycle seems, for some reason, to have a fair chance of being chosen; maybe it is especially salient, maybe the status quo. Then so, in some contexts, do those alternatives that beat x directly or even at one or two removes. But that includes every single alternative if the cycle is all-inclusive and tight.

6.4   ABSORBING OLD ASSUMPTIONS

So far I have used **TS** only to justify the definitions of C and $\succ$ when A is interpreted as a fixed feasible set. In Section 7.2, I shall have occasion to assume it for deductive purposes. If we assume it now, we can deduce **U** and therefore drop **U** as a separate assumption. For if $xP_i y$ holds for all i, then $\{x\}$ is a top set in $\mathbf{P}^{\{x,\, y\}}$, so **TS** implies that $\Gamma_{\mathbf{p}\{x,\, y\}} = \{x\} = C_{\mathbf{p}}(\{x, y\})$, that is, $x \succ_{\mathbf{p}} y$.

It would be eminently plausible to strengthen **TS** thus:

TS+   If α is a top set in **P** *and* in α-twin **P′**, then $\Gamma_{\mathbf{P}} = \Gamma_{\mathbf{P}'} \subset \alpha$.

In other words, if everyone prefers every alternative in α to every alternative in $A-\alpha$, then not only must the social choice come from α (as **TS** says) but preferences between the alternatives below α can have no effect on that choice. But that implies **I**, the Independence of Irrelevant Alternatives, in both the C and the $\succ$ versions:

If **P** and **P′** are α-twins, then $C_{\mathbf{p}'}(\alpha) = C_{\mathbf{p}}(\alpha)$.

If **P** and **P′** are xy-twins and $x \succ_{\mathbf{p}} y$, then $x \succ_{\mathbf{p}'} y$.

For if **P** and **P′** are α-twins (or xy-twins), then **TS+** implies that $\Gamma_{\mathbf{p}}\alpha = \Gamma_{\mathbf{p}'}\alpha$ (or $\Gamma_{\mathbf{p}}\{x, y\} = \Gamma_{\mathbf{p}'}\{x, y\}$). And by definition of C (or $\succ$), that means: $C_{\mathbf{p}'}(\alpha) = C_{\mathbf{p}}(\alpha)$ (or $x \succ_{\mathbf{p}} y \Rightarrow x \succ_{\mathbf{p}'} y$).

So if we assume **TS+**, we can drop **I** as well as **U** in Arrow's Theorem and in our three variants (it was not needed for the Condorcet variants of the last chapter). Although the plausibility of **TS+** makes **I** all the more compelling, I must add a qualification. If we restate **TS+** in terms of utility profiles **u** and **u′**, then the hypothesis that they are α-twins means that their component utility functions *order* α the same way. Like **I**, therefore, **TS+** implies ordinality.

Without finding fault with **TS+**, I shall assume only **TS** in Chapter 7 (and not always there) because the extra power of **TS+** is not needed.

But for now, see how nicely **TS+** lightens the load on those Arrovian theorems:

Assumptions				Consequences, for some **P**
A	**TS+**	$\not{D}$		$\succ_p$ or $\approx_p$ not transitive (Arrow)
A	**TS+**	$\not{D}$	**MR**	$\succ_p$ not transitive
A+	**TS+**	$\not{D}$	**MR**	$\succ_p$ has a top-set cycle
A	**TS+**	$\not{D}$	$(2k-2)$**R**	$\succ_p$ has a top-set tricycle and
				$\succ_p$ has an all-inclusive tight cycle

Distinguished theorists exist, most of them fans of Borda, who dislike varying the feasible set and dislike **I** as well. I ask them what, if anything, they find uncongenial in the assumptions just listed.

7 Strategic Consequences of Cycles

Social choice depends not only on preferences and procedure but on strategy, on how voters choose to act and interact to achieve desired outcomes, and that depends on cycles. Cycles make social choice manipulable: they block any general incentive to vote sincerely and instead create opportunities for single voters to profit from the strategic mis-statement of their preferences. We can generalize that consequence a bit and deduce a more sweeping result about social-choice procedures that are *non*manipulable, or *strategy-free*: if they are not purely dictatorial or preposterously irresolute, they do not exist. Besides ensuring manipulability, cycles block the implement-ability of social-choice procedures by game solutions of the simplest, most prominent sorts: core outcomes and Nash equilibria. Because they are about a fixed feasible set, the promised results are couched in terms of A and Γ. I assume, of course, that $\varnothing \neq \Gamma_p \subseteq A$ for every profile **P** of linear orderings of A.

7.1 VOTE MANIPULATION

A voting rule (or other social-choice procedure) is *manipulable* if it makes it possible, depending on voter preferences, for a voter to profit by mis-stating his true preference. That happens, for example, when a pivotal voter under Plurality Rule votes for his second-favorite candidate because his favorite has too little support to win whatever he does.

The Gibbard–Satterthwaite Theorem is widely but falsely advertised as showing that Γ must be manipulable unless it is purely dictatorial or limited to two possible choices. No. The theorem shows this only in the special case where Γ is *resolute*, or incapable of allow-ing ties (multi-member choice sets). I am now quite old but have never come across a voting rule or other social-choice procedure that is resolute. Ties may be rare under some procedures, but under resolute procedures they are not rare: they are impossible. Ties do get resolved, but then one may wonder what is manipulable, the original procedure – the one we care about – or the added tie-breaker. It is a theorematic irony that Plurality Rule is the most common voting rule in the world but the only way to manipulate it is to make or break a tie, or more exactly, to expand or contract the choice set: if ties are rare, opportunities to manipulate must be rarer.

But dropping resoluteness occasions a problem of formulation. To manipulate, voter i must change a profile $\mathbf{P}$ to an i-variant $\mathbf{P}'$ (they differ only in their ith coordinates) so that $\Gamma_{\mathbf{p}'}$ is better than $\Gamma_{\mathbf{p}}$ according to P_i. Suppose $\Gamma_{\mathbf{p}} = \{x\}$ and $\Gamma_{\mathbf{p}'} = \{y\}$. Then, of course, $\Gamma_{\mathbf{p}'}$ is P_i – better if $yP_i x$. But what if $\Gamma_{\mathbf{p}}$ or $\Gamma_{\mathbf{p}'}$ is not a unit set? In what sense can the *set* $\Gamma_{\mathbf{p}'}$ be *better* than the *set* $\Gamma_{\mathbf{p}}$ according to P_i, voter i's preference relation between *alternatives*?

Because manipulability is only the *possibility* – depending on preferences – of some voter's profiting from a mis-statement of his preference, it is enough that a preference for set $\Gamma_{\mathbf{p}'}$ to set $\Gamma_{\mathbf{p}}$ is *compatible* with P_i. That happens when voter i's beliefs about the resolution of ties, represented by probability distributions over choice sets $\Gamma_{\mathbf{p}}$ and $\Gamma_{\mathbf{p}'}$, give $\Gamma_{\mathbf{p}'}$ a *greater expected utility* than $\Gamma_{\mathbf{p}}$ for some *utility representative* of P_i, some real-valued function u on A such that $u(x) > u(y) \Leftrightarrow x P_i y$ for all x, y. What about those beliefs, or probabilities? Which are the right ones for which voters? Fortunately, it is enough to assume that i has manipulated when *every possible* pair of probability distributions, representing every possible set of beliefs about the resolution of ties, gives $\Gamma_{\mathbf{p}'}$ a greater expected utility than $\Gamma_{\mathbf{p}}$ for some utility representative of P_i. So define:

> An *i-manipulation* of $\mathbf{P}$ is an i-variant $\mathbf{P}'$ of $\mathbf{P}$ ($P'_j = P_j$ when $j \neq i$) such that, for every probability distribution π over $\Gamma_{\mathbf{p}}$ and π' over $\Gamma_{\mathbf{p}'}$ there exists a utility representative u of P_i with

$$\sum_{x \in \Gamma_{\mathbf{p'}}} \pi'(x)u(x) > \sum_{x \in \Gamma_{\mathbf{p}}} \pi(x)u(x).$$

This is one of two criteria of manipulation that Duggan and Schwartz (2000) use to generalize Gibbard–Satterthwaite to the nonresolute case.

The other criterion, favored by Taylor in his 2002 expositions of this subject, says that i has manipulated if he finds the new choice set $\Gamma_{\mathbf{p'}}$ to be either maximax or maximin better than the original $\Gamma_{\mathbf{p}}$: it has either a better best member or a better worst member according to P_i. More exactly:

> An *i-manipulation* of **P** is an *i*-variant **P'** of **P** such that, if b is the P_i-best and w the P_i-worst member of $\Gamma_{\mathbf{p}}$, and b' and w' those of $\Gamma_{\mathbf{p'}}$, then either $b' P_i b$ or $w' P_i w$.

This follows from the previous criterion. For if the P_i-best member b' of one set is P_i-better than the P_i-best member b of another set, we can always find a utility representative u of P_i that makes $u(b') - u(b)$ great enough to give the one set a greater expected utility than the other, whatever pair of probability distributions we may have been given. Likewise for the P_i-worst members.

Recall that the third Arrovian variant gave us a top-set tricycle. From that consequence and **TS** (Top Set Condition), it follows that Γ can be manipulated: *there exists a manipulation of some* **P**.

But we can show a bit more. As explained in Section 6.2, instead of a top-set cycle, one Arrovian variant gave us a top-set violation of $\succ$–**Transitivity**, a top set $\{x, y, z\}$ with $x \succ y \succ z \succcurlyeq x$ – possibly a cycle, but not necessarily. Assuming **TS**, that is enough to ensure that a manipulation exists.

7.2   PROOF THAT CYCLES ENSURE MANIPULABILITY, AND A SLIGHT GENERALIZATION

First a *lemma*: Besides **TS**, assume that no **P** is manipulable – manipulable, that is, by the second criterion, which follows from the first. Let $\{x, y, z\}$ be a top set in **P** with $z \succ_{\mathbf{p}} x$. Then $x \notin \Gamma_{\mathbf{p}}$.

Proof. Suppose on the contrary that $x \in \Gamma_{\mathbf{p}}$. Change $\mathbf{P}$ to $\mathbf{P}^{\{x,\,z\}}$ (move x and z to the top in every P_i, leaving all else the same). Because $z \succ_{\mathbf{p}} x$, we have $C_{\mathbf{p}}(\{x,\,y\}) = \{z\} = \Gamma_{\mathbf{p}}^{\{x,\,z\}}$. Next go back to $\mathbf{P}$ and change it again to $\mathbf{P}^{\{x,\,z\}}$, but now *one i at a time*. Note that $\{x,\,y,\,z\}$ remains a top set at every step, so by **TS**, no change moves the choice set out of $\{x,\,y,\,z\}$. Let step i be the first that removes x from the choice set. Say it changes profile $\mathbf{Q}$ ($\neq \mathbf{P}$ unless $i = 1$) to $\mathbf{Q}'$. If $xQ_i z$, then $xQ'_i zQ'_i y$ (because the change moved y below x and z), so the Q'_i – best member x of $\Gamma_{\mathbf{Q}}$ is Q'_i – better than that (z or y) of $\Gamma_{\mathbf{Q}'}$, making $\mathbf{Q}$ an i-manipulation (in reverse) of $\mathbf{Q}'$. If, instead, $zQ_i x$, then also $yQ_i x$ (else $\mathbf{Q}' = \mathbf{Q}$: no change), making x the Q_i-worst member of $\Gamma_{\mathbf{Q}}$. So the Q_i-worst member of $\Gamma_{\mathbf{Q}'}$, viz. y or z (x having been deleted by this change), is Q_i-better than that (x) of $\Gamma_{\mathbf{Q}}$, making $\mathbf{Q}'$ an i-manipulation of $\mathbf{Q}$.

Because every member of a top-set tricycle is beaten by another, it follows immediately from the lemma that if **TS** holds and if there exists a top-set tricycle (in some $\mathbf{P}$), then there exists a manipulation.

It takes a bit more work to prove the slightly more general theorem advertised in Section 7.1: Besides **TS**, assume a top-set violation of $\succ$–**Transitivity**, a top set $\{x,\,y,\,z\}$ in some $\mathbf{P}$ with $x \succ_{\mathbf{p}} y \succ_{\mathbf{p}} z \succcurlyeq_{\mathbf{p}} x$. Then there exists a manipulation.

Proof. By **TS** and the lemma, $\Gamma_{\mathbf{p}} = \{x\}$. Change $\mathbf{P}$ to $\mathbf{P}^{\{x,\,z\}}$. Because $z \succcurlyeq_{\mathbf{p}} x$ we have $z \in C_{\mathbf{p}}(\{x,\,z\}) = \Gamma_{\mathbf{p}}^{\{x,\,z\}}$. Now go back and change $\mathbf{P}$ to $\mathbf{P}^{\{x,\,z\}}$ one i at a time. Note that $\{x,\,y,\,z\}$ remains a top set at every change, so by **TS** the choice set is always a subset of $\{x,\,y,\,z\}$. Let the ith step be the first that changes the choice set from $\{x\}$ to some other subset of $\{x,\,y,\,z\}$. Then it must add y or z (whether or not it deletes x). Say it turns profile $\mathbf{Q}$ (= $\mathbf{P}$ only if $i = 1$) into i-variant $\mathbf{Q}'$. Because Q'_i moves y below x and z, the original Q_i-ordering cannot be xzy or zxy. So it plus the corresponding Q'_i-ordering must be one of the following:

xyz plus xzy,
yxz plus xzy,
yzx plus zxy,
or zyx plus zxy.

In the first two cases, x, the "Q'_i-worst" member of $\{x\}$, is Q'_i-better than the Q'_i-worst member (y or z) of the new choice set, making $\mathbf{Q}$ an i-manipulation of $\mathbf{Q}'$. In the third and fourth cases, the Q_i-best member (y or z) of the new choice set is Q_i-better than that (x) of $\{x\}$, the old choice set, making $\mathbf{Q}'$ an i-manipulation of $\mathbf{Q}$.

7.3   COMPARISON WITH OTHER THEOREMS

To put this result in context, consider the Gibbard–Satterthwaite Theorem, which affirms the inconsistency of five conditions:

A $\qquad$ A has three or more members.

NΓD $\qquad$ There is no i such that, for all $\mathbf{P}$ and x, if x is atop P_i, then $\Gamma_\mathbf{P} = \{x\}$ (*No Γ-Dictator*).

CS $\qquad$ Every member of A belongs to $\Gamma_\mathbf{P}$ for some $\mathbf{P}$ (*Citizens' Sovereignty*).

R $\qquad$ $\Gamma_\mathbf{P}$ is a unit set for all $\mathbf{P}$ (*Resoluteness*).

NM $\qquad$ No $\mathbf{P}'$ is a manipulation of any $\mathbf{P}$ (*Nonmanipulability*, or *Strategy Freedom*).

The fourth condition, notationally hidden by the theorem's authors and mostly unnoticed by its celebrants, is the bad one. Duggan and Schwartz (2000) reprove the theorem after relaxing that condition thus:

RR $\qquad$ For every $\mathbf{P}$ and i, if all $Pj \neq i$ are the same, and if P_i is either the same as them or else the same except that the top two alternatives are reversed, then $\Gamma_\mathbf{P}$ is a unit set (*Residual Resoluteness*).

On its face this a more sweeping result than the one proved in the last section. My immediate point, however, is not that manipulability is inescapable but that its inescapability is one of the interesting consequences of cycles – and, for that matter, other failures of ≻-**Transitivity**.

In a way, we can turn that around to find a connection between *Non*-manipulability and the *sources* of cycles and other intransitivities. For **NM** has four notable consequences:

$$\mathbf{CS + RR} \Rightarrow \mathbf{TS},$$
$$\mathbf{TS} \Rightarrow \mathbf{I},$$
$$\mathbf{N\Gamma D} \Rightarrow \mathbf{\not D},$$

and
$$\mathbf{TS+I+RR} \Rightarrow \mathbf{MR}.$$

To this, add two implications already proved: **TS** $\Rightarrow$ **U**, and **NM+TS** $\Rightarrow$ **Top 3** $\succ$-**Transitivity**, or $\succ$-**Transitivity** in three-member top sets. It follows that the Duggan–Schwartz conditions (**A, NTD, CS, RR, NM**) imply **AU$\not D$ + Top 3** $\succ$- **Transitivity + MR**, a set of conditions shown in Section 6.2 to be inconsistent.

7.4 CONSEQUENCES OF NONMANIPULABILITY PROVED: THE DUGGAN–SCHWARTZ THEOREM

We have four implications to deduce from **NM**.

1. **CS + RR** $\Rightarrow$ **TS**.

Proof. Suppose on the contrary that α is a top set in **P** but $y \in \Gamma_\mathbf{p} - \alpha$. Let $x \in \alpha$. Construct $\mathbf{P}^x$ so all P_i^x are the same with x on top. Then $\Gamma_\mathbf{p}{}^x$ is a unit set by **RR**. I say it is $\{x\}$. Suppose not. But $x \in \Gamma_{\mathbf{p}^*}$ for some $\mathbf{P}^*$ by **CS**. Let the change from P_i^x to P_i^* put x in the choice set. Because x is atop P_i^x, that change is a manipulation. Hence, $x \in \Gamma_{\mathbf{p}^x} = \{x\}$ after all. Now let the change from P_i to P_i^x remove every *non*member of top set α from the choice set. Then the new choice set must have a P_i-better worst member than the old one, making that change a manipulation too.

2. **TS** $\Rightarrow$ **I**.

Proof. Suppose $x \succ_\mathbf{p} y$ and $\mathbf{P}'$ is an xy-twin of **P**; to show that $x \succ_{\mathbf{p}'} y$. If not, then $y \in \Gamma_{\mathbf{p}'}{}^{\{x,\, y\}}$ by **TS**. Let the change from $P_i^{\{x,\, y\}}$ to $P'_i{}^{\{x,\, y\}}$ add y to the choice set. If $y P_i^{\{x,\, y\}} x$, then that change is a manipulation. And if $x P_i^{\{x,\, y\}} y$, then $x P'_i{}^{\{x,\, y\}} y$ too ($\mathbf{P}'^{\{x,\, y\}}$ being an

xy-twin of $\mathbf{P}^{\{x,\,y\}}$), so the reverse change is a manipulation (inasmuch as $x \succ_\mathbf{p} y \Rightarrow \Gamma_\mathbf{p}^{\{x,\,y\}} = \{x\}$).

3. **NGD** $\Rightarrow \mathcal{D}$

Proof. Suppose on the contrary that some $\{i\}$ is decisive for every pair. By **NΓD**, however, there exist x, **P** such that x is atop P_i but $\Gamma_\mathbf{p} \neq \{x\}$. Change **P** to **P**′ so y is first and x second in every $P'_{j\,\neq\,i}$. In case $y \neq \Gamma_{\mathbf{p}'}$, let the change from P_j to P'_j remove y from the choice set. But the change from P'_j back to P_j restores y and, because y is atop P'_j, it is a manipulation. Therefore, $y \in \Gamma_{\mathbf{p}'}$.

Now change **P**′ to **P**″ by moving x and y up so x is first and y second in P_i. Because $\{i\}$ is decisive for every pair, including (x, y), we have $x \succ_{\mathbf{p}''} y$ and thus, since $\{x, y\}$ is a top set in **P**″, $\{x\} = \Gamma_{\mathbf{p}''}$. Therefore, because x is atop P'_i, the change back to P_i is a manipulation.

4. **TS** + **I** + **RR** $\Rightarrow$ **MR**.

Proof. Suppose $xP[N - \{i\}]\ y$. To show that $x \succ_\mathbf{p} y$ or $y \succ_\mathbf{p} x$, create **P**′ so all $Pj \neq i$ are the same with x first and y second and P'_j is the same as them but with y first, x second. Then $\Gamma_{\mathbf{p}'}$ is a singleton by **RR**, and by **TS** its sole member is x or y. So $C_{\mathbf{p}'}(\{x, y\})$ is $\{x\}$ or $\{y\}$, that is, $x \succ_{\mathbf{p}'} y$ or $y \succ_{\mathbf{p}'} x$. It follows by **I** that $x \succ_\mathbf{p} y$ or $y \succ_\mathbf{p} x$.

Now assume **A**, **NΓD**, **CS**, **RR**, and **NM**, the Duggan–Schwartz conditions. I shall deduce **AUĐI**, **Top 3≻–Transitivity**, and **MR**, proved inconsistent in Section 6.2.

Proof. **A** is assumed, of course, and by 1 we have **TS**, which implies **U**. Then $\mathcal{D}$ follows by 3, and **I** by 2. But **NM** + **TS** $\Rightarrow$ **Top 3≻– Transitivity**, and by 4 we have **MR**.

Because **AUĐI**, **Top 3≻–Transitivity**, and **MR** are inconsistent, so are **A**, **NΓD**, **CS**, **RR**, and **NM**.

7.5 CYCLES AND GAME SOLUTIONS

Perhaps the most sweeping strategic consequence of social-preference cycles is that they block game solutions of the most general sort: *core outcomes* and *Nash equilibria*. To show this, I have to connect Γ and ≻ to games.

A *game*, or occasion of strategic interaction, combines a game form with preferences. In a *game form*, Messrs. 1, 2, ..., n are *players*, who simultaneously choose *strategies* from sets S_1, ..., S_n respectively, say s_i from S_i, producing *strategy vector* **s** = $(s_1, ..., s_n)$ and with it *outcome* ω(**s**) in A. Add a preference profile (still comprising only linear orderings), and you have a *game*. An *x-vector* is a strategy vector (**s**) whose outcome is x (ω(**s**) = x). Sets of players are *coalitions*.

In a *simple game*, some coalitions are *universally effective*: they can do whatever their members all want. Given **P**, we say that x *dominates* y if the members of some universally effective coalition all prefer x to y. The *core* of a simple game is the set of undominated outcomes. In a majority-rule game, majorities are universally effective, so dominance is majority preference, and the core comprises the undominated outcomes under majority rule. Obviously, a top cycle makes the core empty.

We can generalize a good deal. Instead of a simple distinction between universally effective and ineffective coalitions, let us relativize effectiveness to *pairs* of outcomes:

g is *effective* for (x, y) if and only if, for every y-vector s, there exists an x-vector that differs from s at most in coordinates belonging to g.

Now define:

x *dominates* y in **P** if and only if x P_i y for every i in some coalition that is effective for (x, y).

The *core* of **P** is the set of undominated outcomes in **P**.

In the cycle theorems of Chapters 4 and 5, recast in Chapter 6 in terms of fixed feasible set A, the assumptions about social preference, about each ≻$_p$, are eminently reasonable ones to make about dominance in any **P**. That makes the cores of some **P**s empty.

Any proposed *game solution* specifies a subset ΣP of A for every P. The "solution function" Σ *implements* Γ, our voting rule or other social-choice procedure, if $\varnothing \neq \Sigma P = \Gamma_p$ for all P. Therefore, if ΣP is always the core of P and if the dominance relation has a top cycle under P, then ΣP is empty (but, of course, Γ_p never is), so Γ *cannot be implemented by the core* (or more exactly, by Σ).

Nor, more surprisingly, can a Γ that allows top-set cycles be implemented by the set of *Nash equilibria*, where:

> x is a *Nash equilibrium* under P if and only if, for some x-vector s and for every i and i-variant s' of s, not $\omega(s')P_i x$.

On their face, cyclic top sets block coalitional equilibration, the choice of core outcomes. It is less obvious but nonetheless true that they block individualistic equilibration too: if Γ allows cycles, then it must also allow outcomes that are not Nash equilibria or disallow some that are.

7.6   PROOF THAT CYCLES BLOCK NASH IMPLEMENTATION

Nobel Laureate Eric Maskin (1999) proved that Γ is Nash implementable only if it satisfies this monotonicity condition:

MM   If $x \in \Gamma_p$ and if P' is an x-improvement of P, then $x \in \Gamma_{p'}$,

where P' is an *x-improvement* of P if $xP_iy \Rightarrow xP'_iy$ for all i, y.

I shall first prove that Nash implementability implies **MM**.

Say $x \in \Gamma_p$ and P^x is an x-improvement of P; to prove that $x \in \Gamma_{p^x}$. By hypothesis and Nash implementability, x is a Nash equilibrium in P: for some x-vector s and for every i and i-variant s' of s, not $\omega(s') P_i x$. But because P^x is an x-improvement of P, we must also have: not $\omega(s') P_i^x x$. Therefore, x is a Nash equilibrium in P^x as well, and thus, thanks to Nash implementability, $x \in \Gamma_p x$.

Assuming **TS**, to prove that any Γ which allows top-set cycles is *not* implementable by Nash equilibria, it is enough to prove that if there exists a cyclic top set in $\mathbf{P}$, say $\alpha = \{x_1, \ldots, x_k\}$ with $x_1 \succ_{\mathbf{p}} x_2 \succ_{\mathbf{p}} \cdots$ $\succ_{\mathbf{p}} x_k \succ_{\mathbf{p}} x_1$, then Γ flouts $\mathbf{MM}$.

By $\mathbf{TS}$, $\Gamma_{\mathbf{p}} \subseteq \alpha$, and we may suppose without loss that $x_1 \in \Gamma_{\mathbf{p}}$. Now assume $\mathbf{MM}$. Create $\mathbf{P}^{\{x_1, x_k\}}$ by moving x_1 and x_k above everything else in every P_i, leaving all else the same. Then $\mathbf{P}^{\{x_1, x_k\}}$ is an x_1-improvement of $\mathbf{P}$. So $\mathbf{MM}$ implies that $x_1 \in \Gamma_{\mathbf{p}}\{x_1, x_k\}$, i.e. $x_1 \in C_{\mathbf{p}}(\{x_1, x_k\})$, impossible because $x_k \succ_{\mathbf{p}} x_1$.

8   Structural Consequences of Cycles

Besides voter strategy, cycles affect procedural structure, how the process of social choice is organized before anyone gets to vote. One way is by making outcomes highly dependent on the fine details of legislative agendas. That can happen in quite a variety of ways – in the sequence and interdependence of pairwise votes, in the membership of feasible sets, and in the joining or dividing of "questions," or agenda items. Sometimes cycles also turn the apparent asset of veto (or concurrence) power – the power that ties together the parts of government in a separated-powers system – into a liability, a bad thing merely to possess. And cycles create the incentive to form political parties. To show all this, I assume a variable feasible set. That is needed both to study the effects of variation itself and to state recursive definitions and inductive proofs with respect to the cardinality of that set. So results are again couched in terms of C and $\succ$, which we may define in terms of Γ or not, as we please.

8.1   AGENDA CONTROL: TREES

Legislatures proceed by a series of pairwise votes, some conditional on the outcomes of earlier votes. The whole picture of what can happen is an *agenda tree*. For draft measures x, y, and z and status quo (or default outcome) q, here are two arboreal agendas:

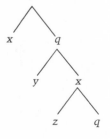
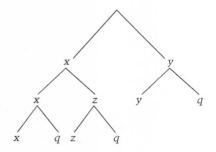

The first is of the sort found in Europe and Latin America: a series of measures are voted up or down until one passes or q survives every vote. The second is Anglo-American: draft measures are compared in a series of amending votes (e.g., y is an amended variant of x, and z another amended variant, introduced only if y is defeated), and the survivor voted up or down. How much discretion would an agenda setter have to determine outcomes? Maybe no single person sets the agenda, but the discretion of an imagined agenda setter is the extent to which outcomes are determined by agenda structure rather than voting.

That discretion depends on the feasible set, on majority preferences, and on how legislators manifest their preferences when voting. Of the two alternatives before him, say x and y, a *sincere* legislator votes for x if he prefers x to y, a *strategic* legislator if he prefers the *eventual result* of passing x now, also called the *strategic equivalent* of x, to that of y. Sincere legislators compare content; strategic legislators, consequences.

To illustrate, here is an agenda tree in which the majority-preferred alternative at each vote is underlined:

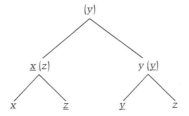

So $x \succ y \succ z \succ x$. Under sincere voting, x would win the first vote, z the second, making z the final choice. But strategic voters would look ahead and compare the strategic equivalent of x at the first vote, which is z, with that of y, which is y itself. They are shown in parentheses, with an underline again showing the majority-preferred of the two. The final victor is no longer z but y, shown as the strategic equivalent of the whole tree.

So how much discretion is there? Assume that pairwise votes are decided by *majority rule* and there are *no tie* votes. Allowing unrestricted agenda forms, in effect binary decision trees, and assuming sincere voting, every feasible alternative that beats something or other can be chosen under *some* agenda on the feasible set. That includes all but at most one alternative. Strategic voting limits opportunities. If there is a Condorcet winner, it alone can be chosen, regardless of the agenda, so there is no room for agenda discretion. But if there is *no* Condorcet winner, there must be a *top cycle*, now redefined in the obvious way for variable feasible sets, and every member of it can be chosen under *some* agenda, but nothing else can be.

Real agendas are somewhat restricted in form and content, especially in the position of status quo q, but the picture does not change very much: under strategic voting, agenda discretion still requires a top cycle, the bigger the better, and it is somewhat restricted only when q belongs to the cycle. To be chosen by some generic agenda, or binary decision tree, an alternative has only to be *first in a path*, a sequence of alternatives in which each nonfinal member beats its successor. That makes it a Condorcet winner or member of a top cycle. But under prevailing parliamentary rules, the path must be one in which q beats every later entry, and in the Anglo-American case every earlier entry must, in addition, beat q.

Here is a real agenda along with a description of alternatives. It was used in the US Senate to pass SB 7, the Veteran's Health Care Amendments of 1979.

c: an unamended bill
a: the bill perfected by an amendment
b: the bill perfected by a substitute amendment
x: a substitute bill unamended
y: the substitute bill perfected by an amendment
z: the substitute bill perfected by a substitute amendment
q: the status quo

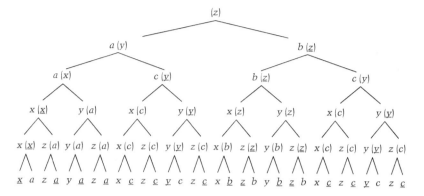

To save space, I omitted the final vote against q by assuming that q would always lose. Let the legislature be divided into three minorities, with the following preferences:

1. $a\ c\ z\ b\ y\ x\ q$
2. $b\ y\ c\ x\ a\ z\ q$
3. $x\ a\ z\ y\ c\ b\ q$

In this picture, left-to-right order represents majority preference except when overridden by an arrow:

Strategic equivalents again are in parentheses, and z is the final choice. It belongs, of course, to the top cycle (as does every alternative but q), and it is first in the path (z, b, y, c, x, a, q). Observe, however, that everyone prefers a to z. A suitable agenda tree, even one that is not truncated in the Euro-Latin style, can impose a Pareto-inefficient outcome on legislators who are perfect, fully informed strategists.

8.2   DENDRIFORM DETAILS

Let me restate all this in a more mathematically exact way. An *agenda* is a finite binary tree. Every *node* has one *predecessor* except for the top node, which has none, and it has two *successors* except for bottom nodes, which have none. A sequence of successive nodes from top to bottom is a *branch*. Such a tree is an *agenda* on α if every node is occupied by one member of α, every member of α occupies at least one node, no alternative occupies both successors of the same node (there is no "*x* vs. *x*"), and any alternative that occupies a nonbottom node on a branch must also occupy a successor either of that node or of a lower node in the same branch (lest it vanish without losing a vote). Yes, even the top node must be occupied by some alternative; an arbitrary one will do.

An agenda *T* may have a single node, occupied, let us say, by *t*. Otherwise its top node has two successors, occupied by t_L and t_R, atop two *principal subtrees*, T_L and T_R. Sincere and strategic choices are defined recursively:

If *T* has one node, $SN(T) = ST(T) = t$.

Otherwise,
$$SN(T) = \begin{cases} SN(T_L) \text{ if } t_L > t_R, \\ SN(T_R) \text{ if not,} \end{cases}$$

and
$$ST(T) = \begin{cases} ST(T_L) \text{ if } ST(T_L) > ST(T_R), \\ ST(T_R) \text{ if not,} \end{cases}$$

Sincere voting lets an agenda setter choose his target from among all feasible alternatives but at most one, the Condorcet loser, beaten by all the others. For if $x \in α$ and $x \succ y$ for *some y* in α, we can always construct *T* so T_L has but one node, occupied by *x*, and $x = t_L \succ y = t_R$, ensuring $SN(T) = x$. Set aside sincere voting: it makes an agenda setter a near dictator, but not because of cycles.

For strategic voting, note that if $(x_1, \ldots, x_k)$ is a path (if $x_1 \succ x_2 \succ \cdots \succ x_k$), and if we add *y* at the earliest position where it beats everything to follow, then the result is still a path, and x_1 is still first unless *y* beats every x_i including x_1. That lets us construct a path on any set by starting with any one-alternative "path" and adding members one at a time. It also lets us combine any two paths $(x_1, \ldots, x_k)$

and $(y_1, \ldots, y_m)$ into one, with x_1 first if $x_1 \succ y_1$: start with $(x_1, \ldots, x_k)$ and add $y_1, \ldots, y_m$ one at a time in that order.

Paths connect top cycles to agendas. Define:

$TC(\alpha) = \{x \in \alpha \mid$ either $x \succ y$ for all $y \neq x$ in α or else x belongs to the top $\succ$-cycle in α (the cycle $\beta \subseteq \alpha$ with $z \succ w$ for every z in β and w in $\alpha - \beta$)} (*top cycle set* of α).

Obviously, every x in $TC(\alpha)$ is first in some path on α, and conversely, if x is first in some path on α, then $x \in TC(\alpha)$. The connection to agendas is two-fold. First, if $x = x_1$ is first in some path $(x_1, \ldots, x_k)$ on α, then $x = ST(T)$ for some agenda T on α. Just construct T in the obvious way:

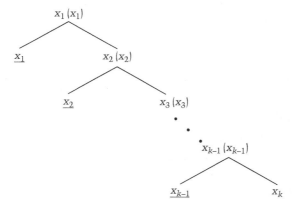

For every subtree T', $ST(T')$ is shown in parentheses; it is the strategic equivalent of the node where it occurs (the top node of subtree T').

Conversely, if $x = ST(T)$ for T on α, then x is first in some path on α. The proof is by induction on the number of alternatives in α. Trivial if $\alpha = \{t\}$. Otherwise, by inductive hypothesis, $ST(T_L)$ is first in one path and $ST(T_R)$ in another. Say $ST(T_L) \succ ST(T_R)$. So $ST(T) = ST(T_L)$. But as we saw, $ST(T_L)$ is first in a combined path on all of α.

To sum up, three conditions are equivalent (assuming no ties):

x is first in some path on α.

$x \in TC(\alpha)$.

$x = ST(T)$ for some agenda T on α.

But these agendas are generic, mere binary decision trees. Their form and their q-positions are unconstrained by conventional parliamentary procedure. By contrast, a real Euro-Latin agenda is a series of contests against q, with no other alternative appearing more than once. And an Anglo-American agenda is any agenda for which (1) each node is succeeded either by no bottom node or by two, (2) in all subtrees T', t'_L is foreign to T'_R, and t'_R to T'_L, and (3) q appears at every final vote and only there. Obviously, any member of $TC(\alpha)$ can be chosen by strategic voting under some T if $q \neq TC(\alpha)$, but otherwise the opportunities for agenda discretion are more limited.

To have $x = ST(T)$ for some Euro-Latin agenda T on α, x must, of course, be first in some path on α. But that is not enough: the path must be one in which q beats every later entry (if any). To see why, go back to the inductive proof that $ST(T)$ is first in some path on α. Because T is Euro-Latin, T_L has but one node, occupied by t_L, and by inductive hypothesis q beats every later entry in the T_R path. Add t_L to that path as before (at the earliest point where it beats every later entry) and q still beats every later entry.

Anglo-American procedure adds a further constraint: besides beating every later entry in the path, q must be beaten by every earlier entry. That is trivial if there are but two alternatives, x and q. Otherwise, the inductive hypothesis implies that q beats every later entry in the T_L and T_R paths and that every earlier entry in either path beats q. If we now combine the two paths as above, then those alternatives that follow q and are therefore beaten by q in either path still do in the combined path, where all others still beat q.

To see the difference between national procedures, suppose $x \succ y \succ q \succ x$. Then (x, y, q), (y, q, x), and (q, x, y) are all the paths on $\{x, y, q\}$. So each of those three alternatives is the strategic choice under some generic agenda. But only in the first two paths does q beat every later entry, so x, y, and they alone can be chosen under a Euro-Latin agenda. And of those two paths, only in the second does every earlier entry beat q, so Anglo-American procedure allows but one choice, y. But of course, it allows more choices when there are more things to choose. For example, when $x \succ y \succ z \succ x$ and all three beat q, the paths (x, y, z, q), (y, z, x, q), and (z, x, y, q) ensure that x, y, and z can all be chosen by Anglo-American procedure.

Although Euro-Latin and Anglo-American parliamentary procedure restrict opportunities, the overall lesson remains: assuming strategic voting and no ties, a top-cyclic $\succ$ almost always allows arboreal agenda discretion, and it alone ever allows any.

8.3   AGENDA CONTROL: SETS

The terms "agenda" and "agenda control" might refer simply to the feasible set and the power to decide what it contains – what is on the agenda. Theorists of decision problems of all sorts usually take the feasible alternatives for granted, but in general it is far from obvious what they are. This enhances the opportunities of critically placed actors to control outcomes, but overall that opportunity depends on how sensitive C is to variations in the feasible set – assuming a fixed **P**.

C is about as *insensitive* to such variations as one can reasonably wish if it satisfies WARP, if $C(\alpha) - \beta \neq \varnothing \Rightarrow C(\alpha) - \beta = C(\alpha - \beta)$. But that is quite a strong requirement, equivalent to strong classical rationality, rationalizability by a weak ordering.

More general and venerable in Chernoff's Axiom, the left-to-right half of WARP:

$$C(\alpha) - \beta \subseteq C(\alpha - \beta).$$

It is this condition rather than WARP itself that is often confused with **I**, the Independence of Irrelevant Alternatives, in part because John Nash (1950) once called it that. Chernoff still makes C pretty insensitive to what is feasible. It says that if we choose x from α and later contract α without losing x, then x remains an allowable choice. However, bearing in mind that $\succ$ is the relation of pairwise choice (**P** held constant), *Chernoff implies* **Acyclicity**: cycles block Chernoff. For suppose $x_1 \succ x_2 \succ \cdots \succ x_k \succ x_1$ and $\alpha = \{x_1, \ldots, x_k\}$. Say $x_1 \in C(\alpha)$. Let $\beta = \{x_2, \ldots, x_{k-1}\}$. Then $C(\alpha - \beta) = C(\{x_1, x_k\}) = \{x_k\}$ (because $x_k \succ x_1$), so x_1 belongs to $C(\alpha) - \beta$ but not to $C(\alpha - \beta)$, contrary to Chernoff.

What if $\succ$ is acyclic? Then every α has an unbeaten member, making it possible for $\succ$ to rationalize C. Not that it must: as we saw in Section 1.1, Plurality, Double-Vote, Borda, and Approval Rules can reject unbeaten alternatives. But if $\succ$ does rationalize C – if $C(\alpha)$ always comprises the unbeaten alternatives in α – then C obviously satisfies Chernoff.

8.4 AGENDA CONTROL: JOINING AND DIVIDING QUESTIONS

A third form of agenda control that depends on cycles is the joining and dividing of "questions," or agenda items: two or more provisions are tied together in a single package, or a complex measure is separated into components. We encountered the former in Section 2.6, in the story of food stamps and agriculture subsidies joined by a vote trade between rural and urban congressional factions.

Here is that example again but with the two measures and three factions relabeled to abstract form from content:

A	B	C
$x\bar{y}$	$\bar{x}y$	$\bar{x}\bar{y}$
xy	xy	$x\bar{y}, \bar{x}y$
$\bar{x}\bar{y}$	$\bar{x}\bar{y}$	(either order)
$\bar{x}y$	$x\bar{y}$	xy

The cycle occurs because xy would win an up-or-down vote ($xy \succ \bar{x}\bar{y}$) but is an *essential package*: neither x nor y would win a solo contest, in the presence of the other ($\bar{x}y \succ xy$ and $x\bar{y} \succ xy$) or in its absence ($\bar{x}\bar{y} \succ x\bar{y}$ and $\bar{x}\bar{y} \succ \bar{x}y$).

The division of questions works in the opposite way. Sometimes a package has to be separated to pass. In its simplest form, this case is like the last but with the positions of xy and $\bar{x}\bar{y}$ – or zw and $\bar{z}\bar{w}$, to avoid confusion – reversed:

D	E	F
$z\overline{w}$	$\overline{z}w$	zw
$\overline{z}\overline{w}$	$\overline{z}\overline{w}$	$z\overline{w}, \overline{z}w$
zw	zw	(either order)
$\overline{z}w$	$z\overline{w}$	$\overline{z}\overline{w}$

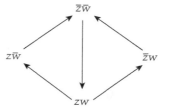

Obviously, z and w can pass separate votes but zw cannot: it is (let us say) an *essential anti-package*. That too requires a cycle, but the reasons are opposite of what they were before: the package (zw) would lose an up-or-down vote $(\overline{z}\overline{w} \succ zw)$ but either component would win a solo contest, in the presence of the other $(xy \succ \overline{x}y$ and $xy \succ x\overline{y})$ or in its absence $(x\overline{y} \succ \overline{x}\overline{y}$ and $\overline{x}y \succ \overline{x}\overline{y})$.

When one minority faction wants one thing and another wants something else, the obvious way to secure both is by joining them in a single package measure. But sometimes the very opposite can secure them too: an anti-package would be rejected as a whole, but its components are separately chooseable. Offhand that seems counterintuitive, and I am not sure how often it occurs, but the famous (or infamous) 1850 Compromise fits my description. To simplify in inessential ways, the US Senate was divided into three factions. Northern die-hards favored z, which (among other things) would admit California as a free state and prevent westward expansion of Texas. Southern die-hards wanted w, chiefly a very tough fugitive-slave law. And Union preservers hoped that zw, Henry Clay's compromise package, would help save the Federal Union from dissolution. But zw would lose an up-or-down vote because the die-hards, a majority, would risk dissolution rather than compromise. It was Senator Stephen A. Douglas who saw that zw was an essential anti-package and secured it by dividing it – something he could do as chairman of the drafting committee.

An agenda can join or divide an issue in several ways. Assume strategic voting, and consider three arboreal agenda forms, each applied to both xy and zw:

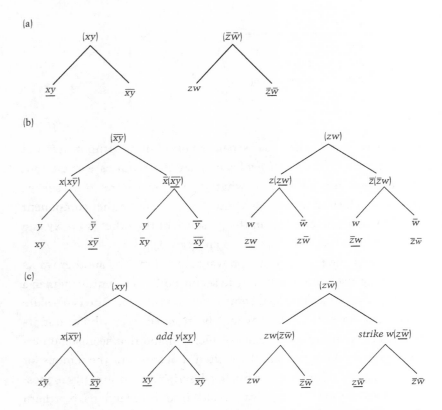

As before, the majority-preferred outcome of each pairwise vote is underlined, and as before, it becomes the strategic equivalent (shown in parentheses) of the next-higher node. Form (a) is a simple up-or-down vote on the whole package. Of course, xy would win and zw lose. Form (b) consists of separate votes on the two parts of the package, with combined outcomes beneath each branch. Because xy is an essential package and zw an essential anti-package, x and y would both lose but z and w would both win. Even so, x and y could win if, instead of voting strategically, A and B cooperated by trading votes. For that matter, D and E could trade "no" votes to secure $\bar{z}\bar{w}$; I wonder if that ever happens. Form (c) has an amending vote followed by a vote on final passage. In the xy case, a package is formed when the amendment adds y to x. In the zw case, the amendment strikes w from the unpassable package.

So packages can be formed or separated by floor votes to amend, but only up to a limit: if we start with zw, an amendment can save z or w but not both. Offhand, one might suppose that a motion to "divide the question" would save zw by separating the essential anti-package into z and w. No. Here is the tree:

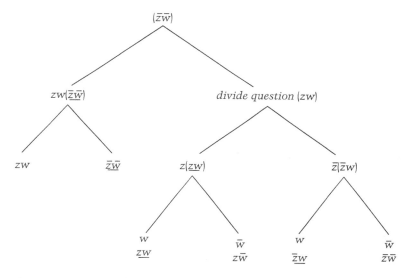

To pass an essential anti-package, the question must be divided *before* voting, not *by* voting. That may be why manuals of parliamentary procedure treat division of the question as a request to the chair more than a motion to be voted on.

To generalize all this, interpret $\succ$ as you please: it is any social preference or dominance relation, not necessarily majority preference. And instead of two issues, each two sided, assume any $k > 2$ issues, the ith consisting of x_i and one or more other positions, including default $\bar{x}_i$.

Let $x_1 \cdots x_k$ be an *essential package*. So no x_i can be chosen separately when all other issue positions are held fixed:

(1)   If $x(x_i)$ is any combination of positions on the k issues with x_i in ith position, and if $x(\bar{x}_i)$ is the same but with $\bar{x}_i$ in that position, then $x(\bar{x}_i) \succ x(x_i)$.

Assume too that $x_1 \cdots x_k$ as a whole can be chosen in an up-or-down vote:

(2) $x_1 \cdots x_k \succ \bar{x}_1 \cdots \bar{x}_k.$

Thanks to (1) we have

$$\bar{x}_1 \bar{x}_2 \cdots \bar{x}_k \succ x_1 \bar{x}_2 \cdots \bar{x}_k$$

and likewise $x_1 \bar{x}_2 \cdots \bar{x}_k \succ x_1 x_2 \bar{x}_3 \cdots \bar{x}_k$

and so on down to $x_1 \cdots x_{k-1} \bar{x}_k \succ x_1 \cdots x_k.$

Add that to (2) and you have a cycle.

Instead let $x_1 \cdots x_k$ be an *essential anti-package*. Now each x_i *can* be chosen separately when all other issue positions are held fixed:

(3)   If $x(x_i)$ and $x(\bar{x}_i)$ are as in (1), then $x(x_i) \succ x(\bar{x}_i)$.

In this case, assume that an up-or-down vote would *reject* the whole package:

(4) $\bar{x}_1 \ldots \bar{x}_k \succ x_1 \ldots x_k.$

Then the previous argument in reverse reveals a cycle:

$$x_1 \cdots x_k \succ \bar{x}_1 x_2 \cdots x_k \succ \bar{x}_1 \bar{x}_2 x_3 \cdots x_k \succ \cdots \succ \bar{x}_1 \cdots \bar{x}_k \succ x_1 \cdots x_k.$$

Observe that in neither argument did I assume majority rule – or much else.

It is worth noting that (2) is needed for cycles, but so long as $x_1 \cdots x_k$ satisfies (1) and is *somehow* choosable – even if it does not beat $\bar{x}_1 \cdots \bar{x}_k$ – it is still an essential package and still unstable: an essential package must be unstable even if not part of a cycle. To illustrate instability without a cycle, suppose we have:

1	2	3	4	5
$x\bar{y}$	$x\bar{y}$	$\bar{x}y$	$\bar{x}y$	$\overline{xy}$
xy	$\overline{xy}$	xy	$\overline{xy}$	$x\bar{y}$
$\overline{xy}$	xy	$\overline{xy}$	xy	$\bar{x}y$
$\bar{x}y$	$\bar{x}y$	$x\bar{y}$	$x\bar{y}$	xy

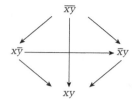

To block $\overline{xy}$, the Condorcet winner, Reps. 1 and 3 might trade votes, 1 voting for y in return for 3's support of x. Absent further trades, the outcome is xy, which 1 and 3 both prefer to $\overline{xy}$. As before, an essential package (xy) is unstable, but in this case the traders are a minority and another feasible alternative ($\overline{xy}$) is stable. In this case, too, xy would not win a pairwise contest with $\overline{xy}$. True, Reps. 2 and 4 could secure stable $\overline{xy}$ with a counter trade. But $\overline{xy}$ is not thereby an *essential package*, for it is also the outcome absent *any* packaging: $\bar{x}$ and $\bar{y}$ would each be chosen in separate, untraded votes.

In that same example, reverse the positions of xy and $\overline{xy}$ in Rep. 5's preference ordering. That reverses every majority preference, making xy the Condorcet winner. Now it is Reps. 2 and 4 who can secure $\overline{xy}$ with a vote trade, but an oddly negative one, an exchange of opposition to each other's favored bills. I wonder if that ever happens.

8.5   CYCLES AND PARADOXICAL POWER

Because everything in a cycle is beaten, and because beaten choices appear vulnerable to revision, cycles appear both to enhance the power to change outcomes and to thwart the power to secure outcomes. Cycles also enhance and thwart power in less obvious ways. Thanks to cycles, a loss of power can be advantageous, a gain disadvantageous.

Often legislation passed by an assembly requires *concurrence* by another chamber or by an independent executive. It or he becomes a *vetoer*. To take the very simplest case, a Euro-Latin agenda requires an up-or-down vote on bill x, and if it is voted down then a second vote on bill y. Here are the agenda tree and majority preferences:

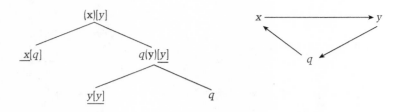

Assume strategic voting. Absent any vetoer, y would win the second vote, making y the strategic equivalent of q at the first vote. Because x beats y, it wins the first vote, which is then final, and becomes the strategic equivalent of the whole agenda. As before, strategic equivalents are in parentheses.

Now add an executive vetoer who prefers q to x to y. If y passed the second vote, the executive would veto it, but we may suppose that his veto would be *overridden*, that the majority which prefers y to q is big enough to do so. But if x won the first vote, it would be *successfully* vetoed because a majority prefers q to x. The strategic equivalents following attempted vetoes are in brackets. The new victor is y.

Although his *veto* (of y) was overridden, the executive's veto *power* changed the outcome from x to y. But it did so to his disadvantage: he prefers x to y. It was a cycle that made it disadvantageous for the executive even to possess veto power, at least in one case. Note that the example works even if vetoes are overridable by simple majorities. Possibly, the majority that prefers y to q is a bare one. When cycles are present, bare majorities can be more powerful in the face of executive menace than is often supposed. And when cycles are present, however high the override hurdle, veto power – or equivalently, the power of concurrence – can be a bad thing merely to possess, even if it is not exercised.

In that example, the agenda was Euro-Latin. But cycles can also create a veto paradox under Anglo-American agendas, such as this one:

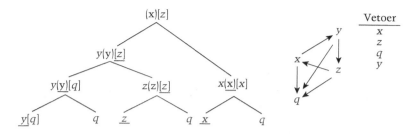

Think of y as a bill, x an amended variant, and z another, introduced only if x loses the first vote. The diagram shows majority preferences, which form a three-member top cycle. Absent any vetoer, strategic equivalents are in parentheses: x is chosen.

But suppose a vetoer prefers x to z to q to y. Then he would veto only y. Suppose too that the veto would stick: the majority that prefers y to q is not big enough to override. The new strategic equivalents are in brackets, and z now wins. But the vetoer prefers x to z. As before, his mere possession of veto power hurt him, and a cycle was responsible.

It is worth noting that the vetoer might be a second legislative chamber, a review court, or even an entire electorate empowered (as in California) to rescind laws by initiative and referendum. A veto paradox can arise whenever two persons or collectivities must concur on legislation and one has a top cycle in its pairwise choice relation. Veto power is supposed to check extreme or untoward acts by pulling opposing positions toward some compromise, or failing that then by blocking any action. But in our examples that did not happen. Nothing got blocked, and far from being pulled toward the vetoer's position, the legislative choice was pushed away.

Similar paradoxes can occur within a legislative chamber. There, cycles come chiefly from *essential packages*, complex legislation whose components have too little support to pass separately. The minority factions who seek those components make up a winning majority, of course, a majority of minorities. It is fair to assume in many such cases that if one of those minorities could somehow be dropped from the winning majority, its favored component would be dropped from the package, making the reduced package less costly to the losing minority. But that is exactly what would happen if those losers shed their voting power by resigning or staying home. So long as the factions making up the winning majority are either more than two or else two but of unequal size, the (or a) smallest could then be dropped and the rest would still be a majority of the reduced chamber. The shrunken majority and the erstwhile losing minority would both be better off because the latter had shed the power to vote. Like veto power, legislative representation is not always a good thing to have.

A more direct analogue of the concurrence relationship between branches or chambers comes from Tsebelis's (2002) "veto players" model of coalition governments: the parties must concur in policy, so each can veto any majority decision. To replicate my paradoxical examples, we must assume (what is not generally or easily observed) that either the government or each of its component parties decides policy by making pairwise choices down an agenda tree, and one whose alternatives form a cycle.

8.6 CYCLES, EXTERNAL COSTS, AND POLITICAL PARTIES

Another structural consequence of cycles is an old paradox used by Nobelist James Buchanan and co-author Gordon Tullock (1962) to show how the external costs of majority rule can add up to Pareto inefficient outcomes. But that paradox is a special case of a more general consequence of cycles: the incentive to form *political parties*.

To simplify the original paradox down to its bare bones, let Reps. 1, 2, and 3 vote on bills *a*, *b*, and *c*, which distribute payoffs as follows:

	1	2	3
a	4	4	−9
b	4	−9	4
c	−9	4	4
	−1	−1	−1

Because each bill would benefit a majority, all three pass. But the total payoff to each legislator is −1. That makes *abc*, the final outcome,

Pareto inefficient: everyone would have fared better under status quo q, with payoffs 0, 0, 0.

To see the underlying cycle, look at the cumulative outcomes and payoffs of successive votes:

	1	2	3
a	4	4	−9
ab	8	−5	−5
abc	−1	−1	−1

So majorities prefer ab to a and abc to ab, but also a to abc. Or if we throw in q, we have $q \succ abc \succ ab \succ a \succ q$.

Buchanan and Tullock attribute the Pareto inefficiency of abc to the external cost (−9) imposed by winners on losers, and that in turn to the use of majority rather than unanimity rule. There is more to the story. Voting coalitions vary in two dimensions. The *breadth* of a coalition is its size, the number or fraction of legislators who compose it. Its *length* is the number or fraction of votes on which its members vote together. In the example, each of the three victorious majorities was narrow because it had only two members, short because they voted together but once. A broad enough coalition – a unanimous one – would have avoided the problem. But so would a long enough though narrow coalition, a two-member coalition that stuck together on every vote. For example, had Reps. 1 and 2 stuck together on all three votes, only a would have passed and Reps. 1 and 2 would have received a payoff of 4 each rather than −1. You could describe that joint strategy as a vote trade (a negative one, to block b and c), but typical vote–trade coalitions are comparatively short: had we added many more votes to the example the problem could well have recurred unless Reps. 1 and 2 lengthened their coalition to encompass all or most of those votes.

Life is short and alliances shift, but comparatively long coalitions exist nonetheless. They are political parties. It is length that distinguishes parties from the fugitive coalitions formed to win single votes, also from those typical vote–trade coalitions. It is length too that distinguishes parties from long-lasting but limited-purpose coalitions – regional and sectoral blocs, single-issue ideological factions, and special-interest organizations (or their legislative captives). They stick together for a long time but only on certain issues. Not that legislators who regularly *vote* alike necessarily constitute a party. Maybe they *are* alike. But parties are *coalitions*, deliberately organized to vote alike. Without coalescing, Reps. 1 and 2 would not have voted alike to reject *b* and *c*.

Once created in a legislature, a party – a long coalition – would be seen as such by voters and would run willy-nilly as a team. But parties need not originate in a legislature. Politicians and their supporters outside a legislature might see the advantage of a long legislative majority, organize an electoral party, and run to become a legislative party. I began with legislative rather than electoral parties because the incentive to form a party, whether by sitting legislators or by prospective ones, comes from the advantage of a long legislative majority. That incentive would be there even if legislators were not elected.

Once a legislative majority has formed a long coalition, the remaining minority might do the same and work to become a majority by luring away some opposition or unaligned legislators or voters. Some election rules (forms of proportional representation) discourage large electoral parties, but the advantage of a long majority coalition in the legislature would then encourage minority parties to form a long coalition *of parties*, before or after election. Each member would perforce become a long if narrow coalition *of legislators*, even if it had originally run on a short platform, as a limited-purpose coalition.

My example assumes that *a*, *b*, and *c* have somehow been presented to the legislature. But long majority coalitions always take control of the agenda so it consists of bills their members can support. Some bills may be costly to some members, but other bills on the majority's agenda would offset their cost. It is easier for some majorities than for others to benefit all its members, of course. Parties therefore attract comparatively likeminded legislators, candidates, and voters – and agenda control makes them look even more likeminded. My example merely shows what could happen were there no majority party or majority coalition of minority parties.

My example assumes too that Reps. 1 and 2 would be stuck with *abc* after the three bills passed, that they could not retroactively replace *abc* with their preferred *a* or *q*. But legislative procedure always makes reversals hard. More important, the rescission of old laws cannot recoup sunk costs: money spent is money lost, and established programs and agencies are costly to disestablish – evidently so costly that antidisestablishmentarianism is the world's most widely implemented public policy.

And following Buchanan and Tullock, my example assumes economically inefficient bills $(4 + 4 - 9 < 0)$ and with them a Pareto-inefficient cumulative outcome (abc). The rationale is that bills are written by majorities, who set their payoffs above a cost-effective level because minorities pay part of the cost. But that was not needed to show the advantage of parties. Change the example by letting the distributions of payoffs from *a*, *b*, and *c* be $(4, 4, -5)$, $(4, -5, 4)$, and $(-5, 4, 4)$. Then the series of majority votes would produce:

	1	2	3
a	4	4	-5
ab	8	-1	-1
abc	3	3	3

That looks pretty good. But as before, Reps. 1 and 2 would do even better to form a long coalition, pass only *a*, and obtain a payoff of 4 each. And as before we have a cycle: $abc \succ ab \succ a \succ abc$.

Inefficiencies are gone $(4 + 4 - 5 > 0)$, but external costs still play a role. If we lower them further, from 5 to 3, the cumulative payoff to each legislator from *abc* rises from 3 to 5, and the immediate incentive to form a long coalition is gone – along with the cycle. Even so, Reps. 1 and 2 would not be hurt by a long coalition if it either disciplined them to pass all three bills or freed their votes on those bills. And if *a*, *b*, and

c were but three of many bills, a party could still be advantageous to 1 and 2.

To generalize all this, suppose that legislative options $b_1, \ldots, b_k$, each the passage or defeat of some bill, are voted on in that order and each would win a nonpartisan vote, but their successive cumulative outcomes form a cycle:

$$b_1 \cdots b_k \succ b_1 \cdots b_{k-1} \succ \cdots \succ b_1 b_2 \succ b_1 \text{ but } b_1 \succ b_1 \cdots b_k.$$

Then the majority, M, that prefers b_1 to $b_1 \cdots b_k$ would be better off coalescing to support b_1 and oppose $b_2, \ldots, b_k$: thanks to the cycle, M would be better off acting as a long coalition. The minority excluded from M can profit from length as well, but less directly: length in opposition can help it become a long majority.

Conversely, the advantage to a majority M of forming a long coalition – a party or multi-party coalition – necessitates a cycle. Suppose, following some vote, that M would benefit all its members if it lengthened itself by sticking together on all or most subsequent votes. But suppose that it fails to do so. Then there must exist legislative options $b_1, \ldots, b_k$, voted on in that order, that win but together hurt M. Because it wins, each option increases the payoffs to some majority (one that overlaps M, as any majority must). So:

$$b_1 \cdots b_k \succ b_1 \cdots b_{k-1} \succ \cdots \succ b_1 b_2 \succ b_1.$$

But because it hurts M, the cumulative effect of those options must be that the members of M are worse off than before. So $b_1 \succ b_1 \cdots b_k$, completing a cycle.

Yes, if the cycle assumed in the first argument is a small one, then the majority that coalesces and elongates need not be very long. But that argument applies to all cycles, big and small, and it is the big ones (which often contain smaller ones) that underly long majority coalitions. How big do they get? As big as parties are long, according to the second argument.

It should not come as a great surprise that without cycles there would be no parties. As you saw in Section 8.4, any outcome for which vote trading is essential must be unstable, and if the vote traders are themselves a majority it must be part of a cycle. But what are long coalitions if not implicit omni-vote trades?

So parties are long coalitions, formed and organized to stick together on practically all legislative votes and to extend their length and protect and enhance their strength through electoral support. Not every party can become a legislative majority, of course, but each seeks to do so, by itself or as part of a coalition of parties. That is because long majorities minimize for their members the external cost of majority voting, the cost to losers. That cost comes from cycles of majority preference between the cumulative outcomes of successive votes.

It follows that the assumption of no cycles would gainsay the incentive to form parties. So, therefore, would the stronger assumption of Single Peakedness, or one-dimensionality, widely found in legislative studies. It is amazing how much scholarship about parties begins by assuming away the reason parties exist.

9 Questions about Prediction and Explanation

Although cycles are not maladies to be prevented or cured, nor misfortunes to be avoided or regretted, they do raise hard questions, positive and normative. The most salient positive question is how to predict outcomes when every feasible alternative is dominated, or beaten by another – how, in other words, to generalize the core to a predictive set that is never empty. Another is how to explain so much apparent stability in the face of cycles – the durability of real social choices. I shall again assume a variable feasible set.

9.1 WHAT MAJORITIES WOULD CHOOSE

What can we reasonably predict the social choice will be in the face of a top cycle, or empty core? To keep things manageably simple, assume *pairwise majority rule* ($x \succ y$ if a majority prefer x to y) and *no pairwise ties* ($x \approx y$ only if $x = y$).

Usually, the outcome is determined in part by election law, parliamentary procedure, and maybe partisanship. But consider the pure version, that of a *majority cooperative game*. There, any majority is free to coalesce around any outcome its members agree to choose, no doubt a member of the core if there are any. The problem is to generalize the definition of the core so it is always a nonempty predictive set. The prediction would be that the outcome – the socially chosen alternative – belongs to that set but not necessarily to any given proper subset. An obvious suggestion is the *top cycle set*, comprising just the Condorcet winner if there is one and otherwise the whole top cycle. An old objection is that the top cycle can be too big. The smaller the set, the stronger the prediction, and as we saw already in Section 1.2, a top cycle can have Pareto inefficient members. So let us start anew.

What can we predict when any majority can do anything it pleases? What set solves the pure majority cooperative game? It will help to let the feasible set vary: we seek a choice set $C(\alpha)$ for every α. Given α, imagine a *recontracting process*: within α, some majority tentatively agrees to support some alternative, say x, but if something beats x then that majority breaks up and a new one replaces x with an alternative that it prefers to x. That process ends, of course, at the Condorcet winner if one exists, but if not then it goes on indefinitely and settles down within some subset of α, where its eventual endpoint is unpredictable.

Call a (nonempty) subset β of α *C-retentive* in α if the recontracting process in α can never lead out of β once it gets in. Before trying to define retentiveness more precisely, let me offer three axioms:

(1) $C(\alpha)$ is C-retentive in α (else we could not predict that the social choice from α will belong to $C(\alpha)$).

(2) $C(\alpha)$ cannot be partitioned into two nonempty subsets, one of them C-retentive in α and the other not (else the process would eventually settle down in the former subset).

(3) If β is C-retentive in α, then some member of β belongs to $C(\alpha)$ (since the recontracting process if begun in β could never depart).

To motivate a fourth axiom, note that C-retentiveness in α was roughly defined in terms of the recontracting (or replacement) relation. What exactly is that? If, among the members of α, y alone beats x, then, of course, y would replace x in the recontracting process. But what if two or more alternatives in α beat x? Suppose just y and z do but y beats z. Then z would not replace x: y would. For the choice of a replacement boils down to a contest between y and z, which y would win. To generalize, say $y_1, \ldots, y_k$ and they alone beat x. Then the choice of a replacement boils down to a contest among them, whose winner or potential winners are the members of $C(\{y_1, \ldots, y_k\})$. That is:

(4)   β is *C-retentive* in α if and only if $\beta \subseteq \alpha$ and there do not exist x in β and y in $\alpha - \beta$ such that $y \in C(\{z \in \alpha \mid z \succ x\})$.

Although *C*-retentiveness is defined in terms of *C*, there exists but one *C* fulfilling axioms (1)–(4). I call it *TEQ*, for *tournament equilibrium* (because any tie-less asymmetric relation, or digraph, like $\succ$, is called a tournament). In short, those four axioms *characterize TEQ*.

What exactly is *TEQ*, besides the one and only choice function fulfilling our axioms? First, define *C-retentiveness* for any given *C* by (4). Then:

> *TEQ* (α)   = the union of minimum *TEQ*-retentive subsets of α (*TEQ*-retentive subsets of which no nonempty proper subset is also *TEQ*-retentive in α).

This definition is not circular. It is *recursive*. For it defines each $TEQ(\alpha)$ in terms of $TEQ(\beta)$ for all β *smaller* than α. That is why I had to let the feasible set vary.

So $TEQ(\alpha)$ is my solution to any game with outcomes in α, of cooperative majority voting (majorities can make binding contracts) without ties. It is not hard to show that $TEQ(\alpha) \subseteq TC(\alpha)$, but unlike $TC(\alpha)$, $TEQ(\alpha)$ is perforce Pareto efficient. An important conceptual problem is how to generalize the definitions of *C*-retentiveness and then *TEQ* itself from tournaments to all digraphs, or asymmetric relations – to the case where ties are allowed, that is.

9.2   PROOF THAT (1)–(4) CHARACTERIZE *TEQ*

I shall prove first that *TEQ* satisfies axioms (1)–(4), then that no other choice function does. By definition, *TEQ* satisfies (4). Because any union of *TEQ*-retentive sets in α must itself be *TEQ*-retentive in α, *TEQ* satisfies (1). And because any *TEQ*-retentive set in finite α must have a minimum *TEQ*-retentive subset, *TEQ* satisfies (3) as well.

The hard one is (2). First, define the *replacement* relation corresponding to any given *C* and α:

$$y\mathbb{R}[C, \alpha]\, x \text{ if and only if } x \in \alpha \text{ and } y \in C(\{z \in \alpha \mid z \succ x\}).$$

So any β is C-retentive in α if $y\mathbb{R}[C, \alpha]x$ for no x in β and y in $\alpha - \beta$. Now suppose, contrary to (2), that $TEQ(\alpha)$ *can* be partitioned into nonempty subsets β and γ so that β is TEQ-retentive in α but γ is not. But $TEQ(\alpha)$ as a whole is, by (1). So $y\mathbb{R}[TEQ, \alpha]x$ for some y in β and x in γ. By definition of TEQ, however, x belongs to some minimum TEQ-retentive subset δ of α. Because $y\mathbb{R}[TEQ, \alpha]\, x$, $y \in \delta$ too. But because γ and δ are both TEQ-retentive in α and $\gamma \cap \delta \neq \varnothing$, $\gamma \cap \delta$ is itself TEQ-retentive in α, an impossibility because $y\mathbb{R}[TEQ, \alpha]\, x$ and $x \in \gamma \cap \delta$ but $y \neq \gamma \cap \delta$. So TEQ satisfies all four axioms.

To prove that nothing else does, take any choice functions C_1 and C_2 satisfying (1)–(4) and any α. I shall prove, by induction on the cardinal number of α, that $C_1(\alpha) = C_2(\alpha)$. By inductive hypothesis, for all proper subsets β of α, $C_1(\beta) = C_2(\beta)$, ensuring $\mathbb{R}[C_1, \alpha] = \mathbb{R}[C_2, \alpha]$. So with α fixed I shall let $\mathbb{R} = \mathbb{R}[C_1, \alpha] = \mathbb{R}[C_2, \alpha]$ and refer to C_1- and C_2-retentive subsets of α simply as *retentive*.

Now cross-partition α as follows:

		$C_2(\alpha)$
$C_1(\alpha)$	α_1	α_2
	α_3	α_4

So $C_1(\alpha) = \alpha_1 \cup \alpha_2$ and $C_2(\alpha) = \alpha_2 \cup \alpha_4$. Because $C_2(\alpha)$ is retentive by (1), never $y\mathbb{R}x$ for any y in α_1 or α_3 and x in α_2, and because $C_1(\alpha)$ is too, never $y\mathbb{R}x$ for any y in α_4 and x in α_2: α_2 is retentive unless it is empty. Therefore, if $y\mathbb{R}x$ for some y in α_2 and x in α_1, then C_1 would flout (2). Hence, never $y\mathbb{R}x$ for any y in α_2 and x in α_1. And because C_1 satisfies (1), never $y\mathbb{R}x$ for any y in α_3 or α_4 and x in α_1. Unless α_1 is empty, therefore, it is retentive, so some member of α_1 belongs to $C_2(\alpha)$ by (3). But that is impossible. Consequently, $\alpha_1 = \varnothing$: $C_1(\alpha) \subseteq C_2(\alpha)$. The converse is similar.

9.3 EXAMPLES AND COMPARISONS OF *TEQ* WITH OTHER SOLUTIONS

The recursive definition of *TEQ* is less transparent than I would like, and its computation is NP-hard, so let me illustrate *TEQ* with a couple of examples. The relation ℝ used in the proof will help. First, note two obvious consequences of the definition:

$$TEQ(\alpha) = \{x\} \text{ whenever } x \in \alpha \text{ and } x \succ y \text{ for all } y \neq x \text{ in } \alpha,$$

and $\qquad TEQ(\{x, y, z\}) = \{x, y, z\} \text{ whenever } x \succ y \succ z \succ x.$

In one example, $\succ$ on α looks like this:

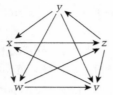

Because nothing is beaten by more than three alternatives, our two consequences completely determine ℝ:

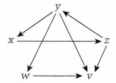

So $\{x, y, z\}$ is the sole minimum TEQ-retentive subset of α, making $TEQ(\alpha) = \{x, y, z\}$.

Besides the core, which obviously is empty in this example, the best-known competitors of TEQ as solutions to tournaments interpreted as dominance in cooperative majority-voting games are TC and these two choice functions:

> $Unc(\alpha) = \{x \in \alpha \mid x \text{ beats every other member } y \text{ of } \alpha \text{ either directly } (x \succ y) \text{ or at one remove } (x \succ z \succ y \text{ for some } z \text{ in } \alpha)\}$ (*uncovered set* of α).

> $Bnk(\alpha) = \{x \in \alpha \mid x \text{ is first in some maximally long sequence of members of } \alpha \text{ in which every entry beats every later entry}\}$ (*Banks set* of α).

In general, we have $TEQ(\alpha) \subseteq Bnk(\alpha) \subseteq Unc(\alpha) \subseteq TC(\alpha)$, but none of those subset relationships is reversible. In the example above, $TC(\alpha) = \alpha$ and $Unc(\alpha) = Bnk(\alpha) = \{x, y, z, w\}$.

Here is a more elaborate example, where, in the absence of any arrow, *height on page* represents $\succ$:

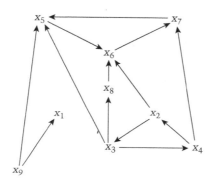

Setting $\beta = \{x_1, \ldots, x_9\}$, we have:

$$
\begin{aligned}
TC(\beta) \quad &= \beta \\
Unc(\beta) \quad &= \{x_1, \ldots, x_8\}, \\
Unc(Unc(\beta)) &= \{x_1, \ldots, x_7\} = Unc(Unc(Unc(\beta))), \\
Bnk(\beta) \quad &= \{x_2, \ldots, x_8\}, \\
\text{and} \quad Bnk(Bnk(\beta)) &= \{x_2, \ldots, x_7\} = Bnk(Bnk(Bnk(\beta))), \\
\text{but} \quad TEQ(\beta) \quad &= \{x_5, x_6, x_7\} = TEQ(TEQ(\beta)).
\end{aligned}
$$

If I have given scant attention to *Unc* and *Bnk*, it is not only because *TEQ* makes stronger predictions but because those functions come with no axiomatic or other strong rationale. Closer to *TEQ* is Dutta's *minimum covering set*:

$Dmc(\alpha)$ = the smallest $\beta \subseteq \alpha$ for which $Unc(\beta) = \beta$ but no x in $\alpha - \beta$ belongs to $Unc(\beta \cup \{x\})$.

In the above examples, $Dmc(\alpha) = TEQ(\alpha)$, and sometimes, we know, $TEQ(\alpha) \subset Dmc(\alpha)$. Quite possibly $TEQ(\alpha)$ is always a subset of $Dmc(\alpha)$, but we do not know. Because *Dmc* is a bit easier to compute, I commend it as a reasonable approximation of *TEQ*.

9.4   A DIFFERENT APPROACH TO COOPERATIVE SOLUTIONS

I have been interpreting $\succ$ as majority preference, but it could be the dominance relation of any cooperative game without ties. In that case, *TEQ* still predicts outcomes, reasonably in some cases but poorly in others. Take the exchange example of Section 1.7. Crusoe has a banana, Friday a coconut. Both prefer an exchange (cb) to keeping their initial endowments $(\bar{c}\bar{b})$. Here are the two individual preference orderings and a picture of the corresponding social preference, or dominance relation, based on property and contract rights:

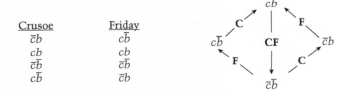

Crusoe	Friday
$\bar{c}b$	cb
cb	cb
$\bar{c}\bar{b}$	$\bar{c}\bar{b}$
$c\bar{b}$	$\bar{c}b$

I have indexed dominance relationships by the relevant coalitions, the one-member "coalitions" *C* and *F* and the two-member *CF*. For example, Crusoe prefers $\bar{c}\bar{b}$ (status quo) to $\bar{c}b$ (he alone alienates his property), and he (or his unit set) is effective for that pair of outcomes because they differ solely in the disposition of his own property.

In this case, even if we close the tie by letting $c\bar{b} \succ \bar{c}b$ (say), *TEQ* $(\{cb, c\bar{b}, \bar{c}b, \bar{c}\bar{b}\}) = \{cb, c\bar{b}, \bar{c}\bar{b}\}$. That seems wrong. Why would Crusoe and Friday not trade? The plausible prediction is *cb* alone. To see why, let us see where recontracting must stop. *C* is effective for $(c\bar{b}, cb)$ but cannot *secure* $c\bar{b}$ because *F*, which Crusoe cannot control, could and would overturn $c\bar{b}$ in favor of $\bar{c}\bar{b}$. Likewise, *F* could not secure $\bar{c}b$. By contrast, *C could* secure $\bar{c}\bar{b}$ (to block $c\bar{b}$)

but *would* not because the coalition *CF*, to which Crusoe belongs, could and would recontract from $\bar{c}\bar{b}$ to *cb*. For much the same reason, *F* would not secure $\bar{c}\bar{b}$ (to block $\bar{c}b$).

As in the picture above, let us write $x - g \rightarrow y$ to mean that *g* is *effective* for (x, y) *and* its members *all prefer x* to *y*. Even assuming that effective coalitions can act cooperatively – as genuine *coalitions* – we can sometimes efface or shrink top cycles by deleting certain dominance relationships, according to this rule:

SC   If $x -g \rightarrow y$ and $y -h \rightarrow z$ but $h \cap g = \emptyset$ or $h \subseteq g$, delete the second relationship (cancel $y -h \rightarrow z$) (*Security Condition*),

For *h cannot* secure *y* if $h \cap g = \emptyset$, and *would* not if $h \subseteq g$. As in the exchange example, that can winnow rejectable members of a top cycle, predicting their rejection. But then it can leave ties, and I have yet to extend the definition of *TEQ* to handle ties. Also we cannot use SC if it rejects every possible outcome, as when $x-\{1\} \rightarrow y -\{2\} \rightarrow z-\{1\} \rightarrow w-\{2\} \rightarrow x$ (in effect a 2×2 game with no Nash equilibrium).

Moser (2012) has generalized *TEQ* so that potential replacements for any *x* are restricted to a "neighborhood" of *x*. One way to define that neighborhood is by excluding alternatives whose dominance of *x* is banned by SC. Obviously, that and other possible neighborhood restrictions increase the importance of extending the definition of *TEQ* to allow ties.

9.5   BEYOND TOURNAMENTS

So allow ties: $\succ$ can be any digraph, not necessarily a tournament. Then there are several natural ways to define the relation of replaceability in the recontracting process. Here are six:

$x\mathbb{R}_1[C, \alpha]y$ if and only if $y \in \alpha$ and $x \in C(\{t \in \alpha \mid t \succ y\})$ (i.e. $\mathbb{R}_1 = \mathbb{R}$).

$x\mathbb{R}_2[C, \alpha]y$ if and only if $y \in \alpha$ and $x \in C(\{t \in \alpha \mid t \neq y$ and not $y \succ t\})$.

$x\mathbb{R}_3[C, \alpha]y$ if and only if $x\mathbb{R}_2[C, \alpha]y$ but not $y\mathbb{R}_2[C, \alpha]x$.

$x\mathbb{R}_4[C, \alpha]y$ if and only if $x\mathbb{R}_2[C, \alpha]y$ and $x \succ y$.

$x\mathbb{R}_5[C, \alpha]y$ if and only if $x\mathbb{R}_2[C, \alpha]y$ and $z \succ y$ for some $z \in \alpha$.

$x\mathbb{R}_6[C, \alpha]y$ if and only if $x\mathbb{R}_5[C, \alpha]y$ but not $y\mathbb{R}_5[C, \alpha]x$.

Define $TEQ_1, \ldots, TEQ_6$ in terms of $\mathbb{R}_1, \ldots, \mathbb{R}_6$ as TEQ was defined in terms of $\mathbb{R}$.

Because $\mathbb{R}_2[C, \alpha]$ and $\mathbb{R}_5[C, \alpha]$ are not necessarily asymmetric, I have included their asymmetric factors, $\mathbb{R}_3[C, \alpha]$ and $\mathbb{R}_6[C, \alpha]$, in the list. Suppose $\alpha = \{x, y, z, w\}$ and $\succ$ has the following form, where the absence of any arrow now represents a tie:

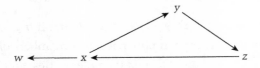

Then $\mathbb{R}_2[TEQ_2, \alpha]$ and $\mathbb{R}_5[TEQ_5, \alpha]$ share this form:

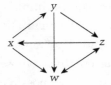

Owing to the two-headed arrow, neither relation is asymmetric. By deleting that arrow, we depict the corresponding asymmetric relations, $\mathbb{R}_3[TEQ_3, \alpha]$ and $\mathbb{R}_6[TEQ_6, \alpha]$, and find that $TEQ_3(\alpha) = TEQ_6(\alpha) = \{x, y, z\}$, which seems reasonable.

But in other cases, TEQ_3 yields counter-intuitive results, as do TEQ_1 and TEQ_4. Suppose $\alpha = \{x, y, z, w, v\}$ and $\succ$ has the form:

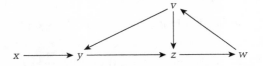

Then $\mathbb{R}_1[TEQ_1, \alpha]$, $\mathbb{R}_3[TEQ_3, \alpha]$, $\mathbb{R}_4[TEQ_4, \alpha]$, and $\mathbb{R}_6[TEQ_6, \alpha]$ have the following forms:

$\mathbb{R}_1[TEQ_1, \alpha]$

$\mathbb{R}_3[TEQ_3, \alpha]$

$\mathbb{R}_4[TEQ_4, \alpha]$

$\mathbb{R}_6[TEQ_6, \alpha]$

Consequently,

$$TEQ_1(\alpha) = \{x, v, z, w\},$$
$$TEQ_3(\alpha) = TEQ_4(\alpha) = \{x, w\},$$

and $\qquad TEQ_6(\alpha) = \{x\}.$

Only $TEQ_6(\alpha)$ is a reasonable solution. But not much is known about TEQ_6, and I have yet to find a compelling rationale for $\mathbb{R}_6$.

9.6   METHODOLOGICAL ASIDES: THE USE OF AXIOMS

Let me add two methodological asides. One is that *TC, Unc, Bnc, Dmc,* and *TEQ* are *tournament solutions*: they depend only on $\succ$-structure. More exactly, a tournament solution, or indeed any *digraph solution*, is a choice function *C* that meets this condition:

> If *f* is a one-to-one function from α onto β and if $x \succ y \Rightarrow f(x) \succ f(y)$ for all *x, y* in α, then $C(\beta)$ is the *f*-image of $C(\alpha)$ ($C(\beta) = \{f(x) \in \beta \mid x \in C(\alpha)\}$).

Part of the interest in tournament solutions – and in digraph solutions more generally – is that they have countless potential applications other than cooperative games and social choice. By contrast, if we start with *TC* or *TEQ* but then winnow some $\succ$-relationships by invoking **SC**, the result is not a tournament solution: it depends on coalitions and their preferences and whether and how they overlap. There is nothing wrong with that, but some generality is lost.

On the other hand, the very generality of abstract tournament solutions can produce results that lack motivation. "Axiomatic method" is touted, but often all it means is that solution concepts are shown to satisfy or violate one mathematical condition after another. Such "axioms" do not form a system that defines a recognizable category of structures (groups, fields, lattices) and lets us mass-deduce theorems true in all those structures. Neither do they yield representation, categoricity, or characterization theorems – the classical payoffs of axiomatic method.

Often those axioms are obtained by relaxing some rationality assumptions to allow cycles, and they have no evident rationale beyond that. Here are two examples:

> If $x \in C(\alpha)$ and $\beta \subseteq \alpha - C(\alpha)$ then $x \in C(\alpha - \beta)$. (*Aizerman*)

> If C' is defined in terms of $\succ'$ exactly as C is defined in terms of $\succ$, and if $\succ$ and $\succ'$ are the same except that $y \succ x$ but $x \succ' y$, then $x \in C(\alpha) \Rightarrow x \in C'(\alpha)$. (Or: If f is a one-to-one function from α onto β, if $z \succ w \Rightarrow f(z) \succ f(w)$ whenever $(z, w) \neq (x, y)$, and if $x \succ y$, then $x \in C(\alpha) \Rightarrow f(x) \in C(\beta)$.) (*Monotonicity*)

But the only rationale that I can discern is rationality: C picks best outcomes in some generalized sense. Obviously, that fits the first axiom, a variant of Chernoff. In the second, the hypothesis seems to suggest that x, already good enough to choose, got even "better" after $\succ$ changed to $\succ'$. Having divorced themselves from rationalizability, certain axiomatists apparently feel pangs of regret.

By contrast, axioms (1)–(4) capture the recontracting idea. There may well be other rationales for other axiom sets that characterize other choice functions. But let them accompany those axiom sets.

9.7   EXPLAINING STABILITY

The second positive question is why there is so much stability. Office holders are elected, serve out their terms of office, and often are re-elected. Laws are passed and remain on the books for decades. Traders rarely renege on their deals. Are no majorities (or other effective coalitions) opposed to these choices? And if some are, why are they impotent?

We must distinguish two kinds of instability. *Latent instability* is the absence of any feasible alternative not beaten by another, as in a top cycle. *Manifest instability* is the actual replacement of a previous choice by a new alternative, as in the electoral defeat of an incumbent, the recission of a law, or the dissolution of a contract. Our negative theorems are entirely about latent instability. What we observe, however, is not much manifest instability, not many manifestations of the latent instability that we have deduced. Why? If cycles led to cycling – to the choice of x over y, followed by z over x, next y over z, and so on – then latent and manifest stability would coincide. But rarely does that happen. Why?

My chief explanation is that social choices do two things: besides filling offices or enacting laws or trading goods, they change the rules of the underlying game by cancelling the right or power or authority to change those very choices, or in some cases they cancel the desire to change them, the preference for a different choice. Either way they cancel the *domination* of those choices. That is clearest in elections. Maybe there is a cycle among candidates, but once a candidate has been elected there normally is no legal way to depose him before he has completed his term of office. The election itself cancels the right that majorities once had to choose a different candidate: the chosen candidate may have been dominated by a rival, but he no longer is, for majorities are, by law, *no longer effective* for the rival against him. True, a parliamentary government (or prime minister) can be legally deposed by a vote of no confidence, and some are, but frequent no-confidence votes prompt new elections that are risky and otherwise costly, especially for cyclists who keep switching sides. In that case, manifest instability is not legally forbidden, but it is *legally penalized*. Often that cancels the *desire* for change: the prevailing government is no longer dominated, no longer latently unstable.

Another clear case is that of economic exchange. In the example of Section 1.7, the actual exchange outcome, cb, was latently unstable: $\bar{c}b$ and $c\bar{b}$ both beat it. But to choose cb was to make a contract that abolished the proprietary rights that had allowed $c\bar{b}$ and $\bar{c}b$ to beat cb. Before the exchange – before the contract was made – those rights made cb unstable, latently so. After the exchange, cb became *manifestly stable* because it was no longer *latently* unstable: no longer was {Crusoe} or {Friday} *effective* for ($c\bar{b}$, cb) or ($\bar{c}b$, cb).

Or consider legislative votes. Once all the pairwise votes are taken on recognized motions, some outcome is chosen, and if a majority opposes it, there usually is nothing it can legally do to manifest its opposition. Parliamentary rules (and maybe informal but well-entrenched custom) make it hard or impossible to put a new alternative against the chosen one in a new vote, at least for a while. Besides those rules, there is the opportunity cost of using up floor time: it would eventually cancel the *preference* of any majority for a different outcome. So, as I have said, would antidisestablishmentarianism, the desire not to abolish old programs and agencies with their sunk costs. And, of course, there is the control of agendas by the majority party or coalition, created precisely to cancel the cost to its members of the partial manifestation of cycles.

Kenneth Shepsle (esp. 1979) has famously explained manifest stability by contending that unfettered majority rule creates cycles, and with them "preference-induced" instability, but legislative rules block their effect, creating "structure-induced" stability (or "equilibrium"). But much of this essay has shown that cycles, although of course dependent on preferences, are not at all peculiar to majority rule or even democracy: they arise under pairwise choice rules of all sorts, e.g. property laws. Yes, certain institutional structures limit latent instability to create manifest stability, I have just shown. But not those structures that Shepsle emphasizes. His favorite example comes from the US House of Representatives, where bills are reported to the floor by committees with narrow jurisdictions and a germaneness rule confines amendments to the same jurisdictions. He contends that those jurisdictions are single-dimensional, blocking cycles. But real bills are not at all like that. They are book-length packages of measures that often enjoy too little support to pass by themselves: they are *essential packages*, hence unstable (latently so).

10 Questions about Prescription and Evaluation

Of the normative questions occasioned by the Paradox of Voting, the most obvious is Condorcet's: What is the best election rule? It is still the chief question that exercises some of the foremost theorists of voting and social choice. Two more questions are likewise rooted in intellectual history, but this time nineteenth-century utilitarian philosophy and political economy – the moral sciences, in the argot of that time: Can social choice be based on interpersonally comparable cardinal utility, or preference intensity? And is social welfare its proper object? Another question is what cycles assume and what, if anything, they imply about the rationality of individuals. A final question is whether, despite challenges to classical rationality, there is a fully general way to do what everyone instinctively wishes to do: make best choices from sets that are somehow unproblematically available.

10.1 ELECTION RULES

We began with a dual problem of institutional design: Condorcet winners sometimes exist but are rejected, and sometimes they do not exist. What voting rule would choose them when they exist and make some sort of generalized majoritarian choice when they do not? Here are six ways to respond to that question.

Way 1. Reject the question. The Approval, Borda, and other rules have their champions, who are well aware that those rules can reject Condorcet winners even when they exist. The case for Approval is that it is especially simple and practicable in not requiring either multiple or preferential ballots and yet it often chooses Condorcet winners when Plurality and Double Vote do not. By contrast, Borda's champions, who offer elegant axiomatic characterizations, are delighted to reject Condorcet winners in some cases. For they see majoritarians led by Condorcet as ignoring important information by caring how many voters rank x higher than y but not how many positions higher. Alas, I see no consensus behind a set of design specifications strong enough to settle the controversy, but I cannot believe that many would follow Borda or Approval by rejecting x, the Condorcet winner, in the second example of Section 1.1.

Way 2. Say what "majority rule" means when the feasible alternatives are three or more and there is no Condorcet winner. A natural way to do that is to ask what a majority coalition could agree to choose if majorities were let loose with no constraint but the feasibility of certain alternatives. That is exactly what TEQ chooses, assuming that $\succ$ is majority preference and there are no ties. Up to a point, then, TEQ might be used as a voting rule. The remaining problem is to generalize TEQ to handle pairwise ties. My best recommendation is TEQ_6. Of course, TEQ can produce ties of another sort: $TEQ(\alpha)$ can have more than one member. But that is true of all voting rules, and as I pointed out, $TEQ(\alpha)$ tends to be small compared with rival predictive-set or cooperative-solution proposals. Besides, it is enough to devise a voting rule that chooses *only* members of $TEQ(\alpha)$: it need not allow the choice of *all* members.

Way 3. Look for the virtues of other, more familiar and more practicable voting rules. Although Plurality Rule can reject Condorcet winners, it supposedly encourages a two-party system, and with it a comparatively clear way to hold the government responsible for its actions. It also depends on ballot information of the simplest sort. The Double-Vote Rule lacks those two virtues, but it may be more reasonable for nonpartisan and primary elections, where two-party competition is ruled out. As algorithms for reckoning the "will of the majority," both rules are imperfect. But they are *not algorithms*. Both work not only by counting votes but by creating incentives for voters and candidates and factional leaders to organize, lead, inform, strategize, make cross-factional deals, and mobilize support. Voters and even politicians know so little about the content and consequences of alternatives, electoral and legislative, that a perfect algorithmic rule, by eliminating the incentive to engage in informative arguing and organizing and dealing, might work less perfectly than those imperfect ones.

Way 4. Take the feasible set seriously. What is chosen from α depends on α, but scant attention is given to how α itself is chosen. Actually, it is endogenous in the voting rule: whether you decide to run for office or introduce draft legislation depends, in part, on the operative electoral system or parliamentary procedure. Instead of comparing voting rules merely according to what they would choose from the same set of alternatives, I suggest we also compare the sets of alternatives that would emerge as feasible under different rules.

Way 5. Appreciate coordination and its arbitrariness. Drivers on the same road face a problem of coordination: on which side to drive. So, we are told, did workers at the Tower of Babel: what language to speak. So do friends who wish to dine out together: where to go. In each case, they seek a common policy to follow. And in each it would help to have a coordinating convention, an established rule that settles the question. In the first case and maybe the others, it does not much matter to anyone what that rule was so long as it was generally known and accepted: its choice was at least somewhat arbitrary. In the third example, the coordinating convention would be a voting rule.

Obviously, it is more reasonable to use Plurality Rule than the opposite (always pick the alternative favored by the fewest voters), but other options include Double Vote, Borda, Approval, TEQ_6, and so forth, not to mention jurisdictional expansion (decide several issues at once, e.g. destination and transportation). Voting rules may be less arbitrary than rules of the road or languages, but they tend to be *somewhat* arbitrary: they are still coordinating conventions for people who have to choose together but do not agree what to choose, and often it is hard to make the case that one rule is uniquely just or correct.

Way 6. See the problem in a wider constitutional context. The effects of this versus that voting rule cannot be compared in a vacuum: they depend on a political system of which each use of any voting rule is a tiny piece.

Plurality, Borda, and other rules by which a single constituency chooses a single representative are rarely used in isolation, to pick a democratic dictator – as the champions of those rules seem to think. Instead, they are usually compounded to choose one party or coalition to dominate a legislature. That is done by election from districts. Then the outcome depends on how district lines are drawn. Suppose nine voters who vote for party D or R to dominate a three-seat town council are located as follows:

R	R	D
R	D	D
R	D	R

If we divide the town into three districts vertically, D wins two of the three seats. If we do it horizontally, R wins two. Offhand the latter seems fairer because the R voters are a majority overall. But to draw district lines on that basis we should have to decide the election in advance of voting.

That problem is avoided, and our original one of choosing Condorcet winners is sidestepped, if we institute the proportional representation of parties. But then we sacrifice the advantage of having a particular representative whose incentive it is to protect local interests and answer citizens' complaints. Mixed–member systems, as in Germany, combine virtues: districts elect deputies by Plurality Rule, and extra seats are then distributed from party lists to achieve proportionality. Either way, a majority party is unlikely, and the problem then is that any bargain to form a government must be made after the election, hence without voter endorsement. The apparent virtue of proportional representation is lost anyway because legislative benefits are consumed by a majority party or coalition, not distributed proportionally, and even the within-majority distribution can reflect pivotal power more than proportional popularity.

Nor do we know much in general about how the several branches and legislative chambers and levels of government, inevitably chosen in different ways by different groups, would vote and concur (or not) and otherwise interact to govern. What we do know is that, thanks to cycles, the power (singular) to achieve goals, or benefit constituents, can be negatively related to the legal powers (plural) of office. Sometimes it is advantageous for one part not to have the power to veto another's actions. The merits of this or that voting rule obviously depend on the wider constitution that it contributes to.

Instead of minutely examining and comparing how voting rules operate in isolation, we should do better to look at whole constitutions. Is there an ideal one? No doubt some are better than others, in general or in various circumstances, but like simple voting rules, constitutions are somewhat arbitrary coordinating conventions: within some range of acceptability, it is more important that we have one than which one we have. Also it is hard to judge them when any given constitution, however durable and however democratic, *could* produce terrible results. That is because democracy is a form of freedom: it is freedom of collective choice – constrained, of course, by some prior choice of procedures. Like individual free will, it leaves voters and politicians free to err, even to make wicked or idiotic choices. Its chief virtue is that, by giving everyone and every faction a voice and the chance to get its way or influence outcomes according to transparent procedures that most people find "legitimate," or acceptable enough not to subvert, it institutionalizes such competition for power as otherwise would occur in a more costly way. That achievement, when and where it is found, is a monumental one compared with the isolated implementation of algorithmically perfect voting rules.

10.2   INTERPERSONAL COMPARISONS AND SOCIAL MAXIMA

Is there anything to the old utilitarian idea that social choices should maximize the sum or average of individual "utilities"? The famous obstacle is the need for interpersonal comparisons of utility, or preference intensity. Arrow gave up utility measures for preferential weak orderings, individual and social, but that did not help. I gave up social weak orderings for acyclic social-preference relations – the minimum needed to maximize, or make best choices – but that too did not help. I even allowed social preference to depend on interpersonally comparable individual utility and that did not help either: the problem has to do less with interpersonal comparisons than with maximization, or the demand for best choices, based on diverse valuations, ordinal or even cardinal.

Instead of asking what our negative theorems rule out, let us ask how and when we do reckon social maxima of a sort from individual "utilities" of a sort. Actually, there are two well-known proposals for doing that, one spurious, the other serious. The spurious proposal is to use the Borda Rule. Look again at this example from Section 1.1:

	1	2	3	4	5	Borda scores:
2	x	x	x	y	y	$x = 6$
1	y	y	y	z	z	$y = 7$
0	z	z	z	x	x	$z = 2$

The excuse for rejecting x is that voters 4 and 5 have a stronger preference for y over x than 1–3 have for x over y. It is spurious because it depends on the feasibility of z. Suppose x, y, and z are candidates for Dog Catcher, but before the election, z finds he is allergic to dogs and withdraws. That makes x the Borda winner. But how can z's allergy have changed anyone's intensity of preference between x and y?

The serious proposal for basing social maxima on individual utilities is to ask people to grade things and then reckon average or median grades. That happens when teachers grade students and schools report grade-point averages. It happens too when consumers rate products and services, say cars or restaurants or plumbers, and consumer guides report average or median ratings. Nowadays such guides abound on the internet.

What is wrong with that? Grades represent judgments of merit, based on imprecise criteria but ones that all judges are expected to use. They are not perfectly objective: maybe they reflect preferences of a sort. But to a considerable degree, what evaluators are doing is offering advice to others according to what they take to be shared goals and standards.

As you know from Sections 4.5 and 4.6, interpersonal comparability, however benign and of whatever source, does not rule out cycles. To illustrate in the case of consumer grades, suppose consumers are divided into five minorities of equal size, who assign numerical grades to five alternatives as follows:

	M_1	M_2	M_3	M_4	M_5
100	x_1	x_2	x_3	x_4	x_5
75	x_2	x_3	x_4	x_5	x_1
50	x_3	x_4	x_5	x_1	x_2
25	x_4	x_5	x_1	x_2	x_3
0	x_5	x_1	x_2	x_3	x_4

Then x_1 and x_2 have the same average grade (30), but how can that make them socially tied when four-fifths of the grading population prefer x_1 to x_2? A *five*-way tie does seem plausible. But suppose we are choosing only between x_1 and x_2 (the two plumbers who can come to our house, the two students who have applied for a scholarship). Then x_1 is the better choice, given our information: merely to flip a coin is to ignore part of that information. But remember: *social preference* is *pairwise social choice*. So $x_1 \succ x_2$. By the same token, $x_2 \succ x_3 \succ x_4 \succ x_5 \succ x_1$, a cycle.

Much the same happens with medians, but because they are far less discriminating than averages, a tie-breaking procedure is needed most of the time. The best-known proposal opts for the smaller median when there are two, and when two or more alternatives have the same median grade it breaks the tie, or minimizes the number of tied alternatives, by discarding any nonmedian ballots along with one median ballot for each tied alternative, then looking for new medians and repeating as often as necessary. But again, that leaves x_1 and x_2 tied although almost everyone prefers x_1. And again, breaking final ties by majority rule, at least when the majority is four-fifths or more, creates a cycle.

Even so, consumer ratings are used by consumers, and GPAs by educators and employers, who demand weak orderings and more: they demand numerical measures. They would reject any guide to restaurants or plumbers or high-school graduates that was presented as a choice function, let alone a cyclic relation of better to worse. One evident explanation is simplicity. Another is that users do not strictly maximize: they combine average grades with other information before choosing, and even then they are willing to choose more than one option (different restaurants at different times, many students to admit to a university). Users also assume that the grades reckoned in the average are from graders like themselves and expect the average to be a good prediction of their own later evaluations, or if not, then they will ignore similar ratings in the future: reliability is testable. But above all they are *not compelled* to obey the ratings: the ratings are no more than guides to voluntary choices.

Grade-based election rules mimic consumer evaluations: whichever candidate receives the greatest average or median grade wins the election. But the similarity ends there. For election rules are not meant to guide voters but to impose a government on them, to compel obedience, to lack any test of reliability, and to reflect radically different goals and criteria and the evaluations of antagonistic as well as likeminded fellow voters. That makes grade-based election rules both unrealistic and exceptionally unattractive when, in a pairwise contest, they choose x over y because x has a slightly greater average or median grade although y is preferred to x by an overwhelming majority.

10.3   WELFARE: INDIVIDUAL AND SOCIAL

Despite these problems, it has long seemed to Arrow, Sen, and other influential theorists that the proper object of social choice is social welfare. The leading scientific periodical of that subject is *Social Choice and Welfare*. To the extent possible, it is assumed, elections, legislative votes, market transactions, and other methods of social choice ought to maximize social welfare, or come as close as may be to doing so. But if social welfare is our concern then neither ordinary votes nor range evaluations nor even interpersonally comparable preference intensities would give us what we want anyway. Philosophers and economists have long made dual use of people's preferences: to explain their choices and to infer what is best for them. "Preferences" cannot bear both burdens. Maybe you always choose a most-preferred alternative. But that need not have anything to do with your personal welfare, with what is good for you. If you prefer a Coke to a Pepsi, the Coke is probably no better for you, and that is not why you chose it anyway: you just like it more or think you would. You might be wrong even about that: maybe the Coke is too warm or dilute or contains poison.

Even if your preferences are perfectly informed, you might prefer what is bad for you. If you spend a limited budget on needed medical treatment for your spouse and forego treatment for yourself, or if you donate a kidney to a sibling, or if you take an extra job to pay for a child's education, you have acted selflessly: you have sacrificed your welfare for someone else's. Likewise but even more so if you risk and then lose your life to defend your country – or, for that matter, to exterminate people whose religion you dislike. You may find such actions gratifying, but we cannot conclude that they benefit you or promote your welfare. Or if we do, then we affirm psychological egoism, the denial of any difference between selfish and selfless behavior.

This is more than a verbal quibble: preference cannot bear the normative burden of welfare. Suppose Crusoe and Friday have contributed equally to the day's catch of fish and have equal appetites and similar metabolisms but Crusoe is greedier: unlike Friday, he is gratified by the mere perception that he has a larger share of fish. Obviously, an equal division of the day's catch would be fairest and would maximize average welfare. But a division that maximized average preference-satisfaction, judged in prospect or in retrospect, would give a larger share to Crusoe. Or suppose Crusoe is a glutton: unlike Friday, he always wants to eat more at a sitting than can be justified on grounds of nutrition, gustatory appreciation, or postprandial comfort, and he becomes very unhappy if he does not get all he wants. Again, a division based on welfare would give them equal shares, but one based on preference-satisfaction would give Crusoe more. Or if Crusoe and Friday are equally strong and skilled fishermen but Crusoe is lazier, we find a similar divergence in the division of chores.

Welfare is closely allied to health, but, of course, it includes such things as education, income, vocational and recreational skills and opportunities, and secure living arrangements – general assets and capacities for living the lives of humans. We call things good and bad not only for people but for beasts and plants and even artifacts (oil is good for your car's engine). Those judgments have little to do with their subjects' preferences, yet they do not seem radically different in meaning from judgments of human welfare. Aristotle had it about right when he saw all judgments of what is "good for" X as based on the well-functioning of X. Not that the well-functioning of humans is so simple or uncontroversial as that of beasts, plants, and artifacts, objects to which we humans have arrogated to ourselves the right to ascribe purposes.

So how and where can social choices promote social welfare? Obviously, some components of human welfare are at least roughly measurable at the individual level (wealth, vital signs, years of education) and the social level too (descriptive statistics on health, safety, and education). Voters and politicians can take account of them and debate their causes, consequences, and tradeoffs: they inform social choosers. Looked at in that way, however, familiar social-choice rules are nothing like algorithms for reckoning social-welfare optima. They are collective forms of freedom, including the freedom to err about what is good for us and (what is especially important) deliberately to neglect or reject our welfare for the sake of other goals. Look at it this way. If some constitution or voting system were guaranteed to promote social welfare (broadly conceived to include social justice, if you like), then there would be nothing to debate, deal, or deliberate about in the electoral or legislative forum: whatever was chosen would perforce be perfect from a social-welfare point of view.

On the other hand, our cycle theorems are purely formal: they do not depend on any interpretation of n, A, or P_1, ..., P_n. Instead of voter i's preference relation, maybe P_i is the relation of x to y when x would be better for i than y – when x would more favorably affect i's *welfare*. Then the cycle theorems of earlier chapters apply directly and show that social welfare is not in general a maximand: maybe x is better for society than y, y than z, and z than x. But if, like Condorcet, we think of basic inputs, called "preferences" or not, as expressed by votes, then "social welfare" is not something that voting rules are designed to calculate anyway. It is something for voters and their elected representatives to debate and bargain and strategize about how to promote and protect and weigh against many other goals before they take final votes.

So set voting aside and imagine a social-welfare criterion, represented by choice function C, that is purely objective, or independent of preferences, except for one qualification: any chosen alternative must be Pareto optimal. To minimize possible sources of cycles, assume a linear ordering W of A for making objective welfare comparisons. Then $C(\alpha)$ consists of the W-best Pareto optimal alternative in α. Now let $xWyWz$ and suppose some individuals prefer z to x to y, the rest, y to z to x. Because everyone prefers z to x, the Pareto set from $\{x, z\}$ is $\{z\}$, so $C(\{x, z\}) = \{z\}$. But the Pareto set from $\{x, y\}$ is $\{x, y\}$ itself, so $C(\{x, y\}) = \{x\}$ inasmuch as xWy. Likewise, $C(\{y, z\}) = \{y\}$. That is, $z \succ x \succ y \succ z$. The apparently modest constraint of Pareto optimality is enough to turn an objective welfare ordering into a cycle. Social welfare may not have much to do with individual preferences, but cycles are hard to escape.

10.4   ASSUMPTIONS AND IMPLICATIONS ABOUT
INDIVIDUAL RATIONALITY

To prove what we have about *social*-preference cycles, what did we assume and what did we have to assume about *individual* preferences? And what, if anything, can we infer about those preferences? Must they meet the conventional conditions of rationality?

We assumed, of course, that voters have preference relations on A. Let Δ be the set of possible ones. So Δ^n, the set of ordered n-tuples of members of Δ, comprises those preference profiles $\mathbf{P} = (P_1, \ldots, P_n)$ etc. for which $\succ_{\mathbf{p}}$ is defined. Arrow let Δ be the set of *weak orderings* of A. Except in the theorem of Sections 5.4 and 5.5, I have restricted Δ to *linear* orderings. Although that strengthened $\mathbf{D}$ and $\mathbf{U}$ a tiny bit, it simplified proofs, and overall it strengthened the theorems of Chapters 3, 4, and 6: if cycles can occur in the restricted universe of linear preferences, they can occur in any wider universe.

I could have strengthened those results further in the same direction. For example, to prove that some $\mathbf{P}$ has a top tri-cycle, I obviously could have assumed, for every three-member α and linear ordering λ of α, that there exists a P in Δ such that P is an asymmetric relation on A, $\lambda \subseteq P$, and xPy for all x in α and y in $A - \alpha$. That accommodates the possibility that voters cannot distinguish more than a few levels of preference. None of this means that any of those restrictions on voter preferences are "correct," either factually or normatively. They are "even if" restrictions: *even if* voter preferences are restricted in those tough ways, social preference can still be cyclic.

But what happens if we relax those restrictions a tiny bit? Classical rationality requires weak preference orderings, and that is tantamount to the transitivity of preference and indifference. An old criticism is that the transitivity of indifference can easily break down, as when $xIyIzPx$ because two differences that fall beneath a threshold of discernibility add up to a discernible difference (between x and z). A particularly modest relaxation of the weak-ordering or linear-ordering requirement, which allows a few such examples, says simply that if x, y, z are any three alternatives, then Δ contains a relation P such that $xIyIzPx$ and P ranks x, y, z above all other alternatives.

Add that assumption to $\mathbf{A}$, $\mathbf{U^+}$, and "$n \geq 3$," and it follows almost immediately that **Acyclicity** is false: some $\mathbf{P}$ makes $\succ_\mathbf{p}$ cyclic. For our assumption about Δ lets construct a $\mathbf{P}$ of the following form:

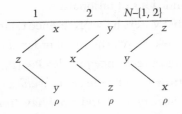

where ρ is some acceptable preference relation on $A - \{x, y, z\}$ and those lines stand for indifference (e.g., xI_1zI_1yIx although $xP_1 y$). Thanks to $\mathbf{U^+}$, $x \succ_\mathbf{p} y \succ_\mathbf{p} z \succ_\mathbf{p} x$ and all three alternatives beat everything else – a top-set tri-cycle. The assumption of perfect individual rationality, including the transitivity of indifference, just made our earlier results harder to prove: they were "even if" assumptions.

Those findings are implicit critiques of individual rationality – or the conventional criteria thereof. For we are free to reinterpret $\succ_\mathbf{p}$ as one individual's preference relation based on multiple orderings $P_1, \ldots, P_n$. The latter might simply be the preference orderings of other individuals – his family, countrymen, customers, electoral constituents, or whatnot. Or we can read $P_1, \ldots, P_n$ as rankings according to some n criteria. If, for example, A comprises cars, the criteria might be speed, safety, comfort, and resale value. Instead of criteria, we can speak of factors, dimensions, considerations, objectives, or even states of nature.

In many cases, it is reasonable to suppose that only ordinal information is available. A car buyer who is not a car buff, and even one who is, is not likely to be able to judge, for example, that the superiority of car x over car y in comfort is 3.7 times the superiority of y over x in speed, or to make tradeoffs between comfort and speed as though substituting a quart of milk for a certain number of eggs. But just in case such intercriterial cardinal comparisons are available, we have the cycle theorem of Section 4.6.

At bottom, individuals do not differ that much from societies. Internally, we are not such absolute monarchies that we can compare and choose without convening mental parliaments of criteria. The Paradox of Voting warned us against anthropomorphizing societies. It should warn us, too, against unitizing people. Man is indeed a social animal. Does it follow that he is not a *rational* animal? In a conventional sense, yes. But in saying so I mean to refute conventional rationality as a norm: there is nothing wrong with a cyclic preference or a choice function that cannot be rationalized.

10.5 BEST CHOICES FROM CHOSEN SETS

The cycles discovered by Condorcet are not peculiar to exotic combinations of voter preferences. Neither are they peculiar to majority rule, to voting, or even to social as opposed to individual choice procedures. Why, then, do we find it so natural to seek best choices, to predict and prescribe outcomes that would survive pairwise comparison with every rival? It is hard even to introduce Condorcet's second discovery without immediately contradicting it by asking what is the *best* way to make choices in the face of cycles.

This puzzle is tied to another, touched upon earlier: how to choose the set from which to choose. Offhand, telling us what to choose from a given set without saying how to choose that set is like giving us half the recipe for baking a cake. Which set of alternatives qualifies as the feasible set on any given occasion? When feasible sets are best defined and easiest to find, that is usually partway through a choice process, one that begins with legislative agenda setting or the nomination of electoral candidates or some such thing. But with what set does it all begin?

Feasible sets make cycles matter. Suppose x is preferred (individually or socially) to y, y to z, z back to x, and w to all three. Then there is no instability if the feasible alternatives are, for example, x and y, or x, y, z, and w, but there is if they are x, y, and z.

Cycles make feasible sets matter more: they make C more sensitive to what is feasible. C is about as insensitive as one can reasonably demand if it satisfies WARP: unless $C(\alpha) - \beta$ is empty, it equals $C(\alpha - \beta)$. But that is tantamount to strong rationality, rationalizability by a weak ordering. And as you saw in Section 8.3, even the left-to-right half of WARP $(C(\alpha) - \beta \subseteq C(\alpha - \beta))$ implies Acyclicity.

In choosing the set from which to choose, we seek choice options that are mutually exclusive, jointly exhaustive, and singly feasible. For that, they do not have to be very specific. I might say that you can buy a car or not but omit makes and models, or list makes and models but omit price, color, time of purchase, and much more – not to mention the various ways of not buying a car, such as stealing one. Obviously, many choices, individual and social, are like that. They are chosen from among options that are few and not very specific, but perforce mutually exclusive and jointly exhaustive (buy a car or not). Whether each is feasible is another matter (maybe you are legally barred from owning a car). The simplest of those choices are pairwise (buy a car or not, run for Congress or not, go to war or not). Such choices may be less specific than one would like, but when the options are two they create no cycles. And because they are broad categories of objects or events, we can choose one and make it ever more specific by choosing between subcategories, then sub-subcategories, and so on. Each successive categorial choice and its partition in two creates a new, smaller set from which to make an even more specific choice.

Let Π be the relation of preference, or pairwise choice, between disjoint categories. We must assume, then, that Π is a relation between finite, nonempty subsets of A and that $\alpha\Pi\beta$ implies $\alpha\cap\beta = \varnothing$. Beyond that it is reasonable to connect Π to C (of which, as always, $\varnothing \neq C(\alpha) \subseteq \alpha$) with three axioms:

(1) If $\alpha \subset \beta$ and $\alpha\Pi\beta - \alpha$, then $C(\alpha) \subseteq C(\beta) \neq \beta$.

(2) If $C(\beta) \neq \beta$, then $C(\beta)\Pi\beta - C(\beta)$.

(3) $C(\beta) = C(C(\beta))$.

Suppose we have partitioned a restaurant menu (β) into meat and seafood dishes (α and β – α) and we prefer meat (αΠβ – α). Then, says (1), we may set seafood aside and narrow our final choice to meat ($C(α) ⊆ C(β)$) and we ought to narrow it somehow ($C(β) ≠ β$). Axioms (2) and (3) just say that, as categories of menu items go, choice set $C(β)$ is the best: it is better than the rest ($C(β)Πβ – C(β)$ unless $C(β) = β$) and it cannot be improved ($C(β) = C(C(β))$).

Objection: Suppose each alternative x has utility $u(x)$ and $C(α)$ always picks the best member or members of α ($C(α) = \{x ∈ α \mid u(x) ≥ u(y)$ for all y in α\}). Let $u(a) = 5$, $u(b) = 10$, and $u(c) = –100$. Then if Π compares sets by their average utilities, we have $\{a\}Π\{a, b, c\} – \{a\}$ but $C(\{a\}) = \{a\} ⊆ C(\{a, b, c\}) = \{b\}$, contrary to (1).

Reply: Π does not mean greater to less in average utility. Instead, like any preference relation, it is a species of pairwise choice, now of the categorial variety: assuming $α ⊆ β$, $αΠβ – α$ means that α may be chosen in preference to the rest of β – that the choice from β may be narrowed to α.

Objection: The axioms presuppose an underlying feasible set (β) of maximally specific alternatives. How is it found?

Reply: The members of A, and therefore of each β, can be as specific or nonspecific as one likes. Real alternatives are rarely if ever perfectly specific – whatever that might mean. Draft laws are always couched in somewhat general terms, and electoral candidates may look like concrete quantities of protoplasm but what they offer voters are general promises and maybe attitudes, skills, and character traits. More important, we do not always have to know much about β to begin the process of nonspecific choice, of choice by categories. In the menu case, we might be able (depending on details of the case) to compare the general categories of meat and seafood dishes without knowing exactly which of either are on the menu (β). All we absolutely have to know is that both are feasible. That means their intersections with β are nonempty – though successive refinements require ever more knowledge of that sort. As for β itself, it is not so much found as created, if not by some official procedure of ballot or agenda inclusion, then by our somewhat arbitrary decision to choose and refine and stop refining categories.

In one way, Axioms (1)–(3) are not at all restrictive. Take any choice function C. If it does not already satisfy (3) (idempotency), we can tighten it to a function F that does: just let $F(\alpha) \equiv$ the $\subseteq$-least member of the $\subseteq$-least family containing α and closed under C. So we may as well assume that C itself satisfies (3). But then it is trivial that there exists a relation Π which, together with C, satisfies (1)–(3): just define Π so that $\alpha\Pi\beta$ if and only if $\alpha\cap\beta = \varnothing$ and $C(\alpha\cup\beta) = \alpha$. True, that is not a very interesting interpretation of Π, but my immediate point is merely that (1)–(3) do not restrict C if we do not care what relation gets plugged in for Π.

But if we do care, then Axioms (1)–(3) are as restrictive as can be short of inconsistency. Given any Π – any way of making pairwise comparisons between disjoint categories – there exists at most one choice function satisfying (1)–(3).

Proof. Let C_1 and C_2 be any choice functions satisfying (1)–(3). I shall deduce, by induction on the cardinality of β, that $C_1(\beta) = C_2(\beta)$.

Suppose not. So $C_1(\beta)$ and $C_2(\beta)$ cannot both equal β. Say $C_1(\beta) \neq \beta$ and thus $C_1(\beta) \subset \beta$. Then $C_1(\beta)\Pi\beta - C_1(\beta)$ by (2). So if we put C_2 for C and $C_1(\beta)$ for α in (1), we have

(4) $C_2(C_1(\beta)) \subseteq C_2(\beta) \neq \beta$.

Therefore, $C_1(\beta)$ and $C_2(\beta)$ are both different from β, hence both smaller than β. But

$$
\begin{aligned}
C_1(\beta) &= C_1(C_1(\beta)) && \text{by (3)} \\
&= C_2(C_1(\beta)) && \text{by inductive hypothesis} \\
&\subseteq C_2(\beta) && \text{by (4).}
\end{aligned}
$$

The converse is similar.

Once tightened, every C satisfies (1)–(3) for some Π. But we have just proved that every reasonable Π (every Π that satisfies (1)–(3) for some C) determines a unique C satisfying (1)–(3) . That makes every choice process reducible to pairwise comparisons, or preferences, between categories of varying specificity. Regardless of the content of C, (1)–(3) tell us that C makes best choices in a generalized sense. And regardless of the content of C, we can always arrive at $C(\beta)$ or a subset thereof by choosing categories that win pairwise comparisons with all rivals. But that is tantamount to choosing the set from which to choose – and doing so over and over as desired. Our deeply held conviction that it is always possible to choose a set from which to choose and then make a best choice from it can be construed, after all, as compatible with any choice process, however bizarre or cycle prone.

Cycles intrude as follows. Once we have chosen a category and successively refined it to any desired degree of specificity, we can in principle go back and find equally specific refinements of all categorial options rejected along the way, then compare our final choice with each of them one at a time. It might not survive every comparison. It will not if it is part of a cycle.

The limits of what we have found are worth emphasizing. We can always choose between categories that are perforce mutually exclusive and jointly exhaustive and do so over and over with subcategories, but of course we have no general guarantee that all those categories and subcategories are singly feasible. We can in principle reduce any choice process to pairwise comparisons, but that does not tell us how in practice to make those comparisons. It would be worth investigating which sorts of Π relation determine choice functions of this or that sort, say rationalizable ones. The reason I have emphasized preference rather than choice, Π relations rather than C functions, is that every idempotent choice function satisfies (1)–(3) for *some* Π.

Concluding Caveats

Cycles and instability are neither good nor bad. What is bad is to misinterpret them as anomalies to be assumed away, antinomies to be explained away, or misfortunes to be wished away. What is good is to appreciate how common and varied their sources and consequences are. It is good because cycles tie together a variety of independently interesting aspects of social choice.

Let me end with twenty caveats against oversights and errors mentioned earlier but so common they merit emphasis.

Neither the Voting Paradox nor Arrow's Impossibility Theorem reveals an "inconsistency" or "incoherence" of any sort – except, of course, that the existence of a cycle or other intransitivity is inconsistent with the assumption that there is none.

The near certainty of instability in a space of two or more dimensions is supposed to be hard to prove and to contrast sharply with Black's simple stability theorem for one dimension, but actually it is a trivial consequence of Black's theorem.

Although a limit on what can be proved, that same result is not much of a limit on the incidence of stability in the real world, for it rests on an extremely restrictive assumption. Instability based on essential packaging does not. Neither does it depend on majority rule or much else.

Far from being exotic or contentious, examples of cycles based on individual rights are as common as trade.

Arrow's Theorem says nothing about cycles or even nontransitive social preference.

Arrow's background assumptions, including **I**, the Independence of Irrelevant Alternatives, are quite unrestrictive, remarkable only as magnets of misconstruction. A vast amount of argle-bargle to the contrary rests on demonstrably erroneous readings.

A modest addition to Arrow's background assumptions does yield a cycle, but it is not the meretricious Positive Responsiveness. The Arrovian cycle theorem based on the latter assumption shows how easy it is to get away with superficially attractive falsehood.

The shortest route to the most general possible structural condition for cycles runs not through Arrow but through Condorcet. Even the proof directly generalizes Condorcet's latin-square example.

Manipulability is one of the consequences of cycles, a fact that can be generalized a bit and used as a lemma to prove the general inescapability of manipulability. A famous purported proof foundered on a false premise, Resoluteness.

The failure of implementability by the core is obviously a consequence of cycles, but so, less obviously, is the failure of implementability by the set of Nash equilibria.

Cycles underly not only the incentive to combine legislative items – to trade votes or write complex bills – but to divide them.

Thanks to cycles, it can be disadvantageous merely to possess veto power. So the requirement of concurrence between parts of government does not always create a balance or compromise of interests, and the formal power to veto can lessen the real power to achieve goals. It is a mistake, therefore, to reckon "power" by adding "powers" – as some scholars have tried to do.

Without cycles, there would be no political parties, important because a great deal of scholarship about parties assumes away cycles by assuming Single Peakedness: that assumes away parties.

In the quest for a solution concept tolerant of cycles, it is misleading to invoke axioms that merely look good or enjoy a loose rationale based on classical rationality.

When explaining observed stability, it is a mistake not to distinguish latent from manifest instability, and another mistake to seek subtle procedural peculiarities instead of looking at something that social choices of all sorts almost always do: besides picking one alternative over others, they change the underlying game by cancelling either the power or the desire to choose other alternatives.

When picking a voting rule, one should look not only at how it calculates choices from votes but at the strategic incentives it creates, at its wider constitutional context, at the feasible sets that arise in response to its use, at its coordinating role, and above all at whether it contributes to institutionalizing those changes of policy and regime that otherwise would occur in more costly ways.

The ways in which we measure individual preferences in order to reckon aggregate preference may serve their purpose well, but that purpose is not to aggregate antagonistic preferences or to govern the subjects of those preferences.

Social-choice procedures are not and cannot be algorithms for finding social-welfare optima or, more broadly, for rendering automatic judgments about what is good or bad for society. Even individual welfare is not based on preferences. Like peace, justice, and freedom, social welfare may be a legitimate goal or social value, but its achievement is something to be argued about, maybe weighed against other goals or values, and voted on by citizens and legislators. It cannot be the infallible product of their votes, whatever those votes happen to be, else they could not deliberate and disagree about it.

It may be true, as some have contended, that rationality cannot be attributed to whole societies or their choices or their public procedures. But then, and for much the same reasons, it cannot be attributed to individual persons or their choices or their mental processes.

How to choose a set of alternatives from which to make a best choice depends on how specific a choice one chooses to make.

Underbook: Background and Sources by Chapter

CHAPTER I

Condorcet's contribution is from his 1785 *Essai*. Borda (1781) had proffered his Rule and appreciated the rejection by Plurality Rule of Condorcet winners (to name them anachronistically). See Black (1958, Part II), McLean and Urken (1995), and Gehrlein (2006, Chapter 1) for early history (for more recent history, those works are less reliable). The Approval Rule comes from Brams and Fishburn (1978).

May (1954) and McGarvey (1953) proved their well-known theorems, of course, but my treatments take small liberties to simplify formulation and proofs; in May's case, I omitted needless notation and relaxed his third assumption.

Further discussed in Chapter 5, **VU** (my name for it) and the $n \times n$ example originated with Ward (1960). The Liberal Paradox is from Sen (1970a); see also his (1970b, Chapters 6, 6*). The idea that every humdrum economic exchange creates a cycle is from my 1981 article; see also my 1986 book, pp. 261f.

CHAPTER 2

Black (1948) defined Single Peakedness and proved his median-stability theorem; see also his 1958 book. The strengthened variant of Single Peakedness, also called the one-dimensional spatial model of voting, is often strengthened further by making voter preferences depend solely on distance from favorite points, regardless of left or right direction. In that form, it comes from Hotelling (1929) and was popularized by Downs (1957). Both added a game between two mobile competitors, each seeking a majority of votes by taking positions on the line, and noted that their positions would converge to the median.

The generalizations of Single Peakedness, weaker sufficient conditions for stability, are from Sen and Pattanaik (1969), Inada (1969), Pattanaik (1971), and Fishburn (1973, Chapters 8–11). Condorcet Freedom, which further generalizes all those conditions, is from my 1986 book, pp. 96–99.

The fully general form of the spatial model comes from Plott (1967), generalizing Davis and Hinich (1966) and ultimately Black and Newing (1951); see also Enelow and Hinich 1984. 360 Degree Medianhood comes from my 2011 article, and before that my printed class notes over the years, but priority of publication goes to Cox (1987). The name and the connections to Black and Plott are new.

My generalization of 360 Degree Medianhood beyond simple-majority rule was paralleled for Pairwise Symmetry by McKelvey and Schofield (1987). Hammond and Miller (1987) first pointed out the potential stabilizing effect of the concurrent-majority rule.

Romer and Rosenthal (1978) famously saw that even outrageous legislation is sometimes majority-preferred to bad enough default alternatives, ones distant from the status quo. By contrast, Krehbiel (1998) saw how hard it is to defeat reasonable status quos using the combination of concurrence and super-majority requirements of the US Congress. Both contributions assumed a single dimension, but needlessly so. In one dimension or more, popularity of the default outcome really matters.

The Congressional vote-trade story is from Ferejohn (1985). In its general form, the essential-package result comes from my 1981 article, where I affirmed its triviality but still festooned it with too much notation. Downs (1957, pp. 55–69) first saw that a majority of minorities would produce an unstable choice. This was rediscovered and stated more formally by Kadane (1972), Oppenheimer (1975), and Bernholz (1973), then generalized by Bernholz (1974) and further generalized by myself (1977 and esp. 1981).

The original theorem of McKelvey (1976) about an all-inclusive cycle rested on a highly restrictive assumption about voter preferences, relaxed by Schofield (1978); Schofield further showed that the global cycle can be broken down into local cycles.

The exceptionally influential (NOMINATE) method of dimensional analysis device comes from Poole and Rosenthal (1985, 1997). My 2011 article shows that legislative histories almost never confirm or refute stability but almost always refute Single Peakedness. See also Koford (1989) on the problem of observing dimensionality.

CHAPTER 3

On rational choice functions and WARP, see Arrow (1959). Arrow's Theorem comes from his 1950 article, his 1952 book, and its 1963 revision, which left the original book intact but added Chapter 8. The 1950/52 proof had an error discovered by Blau (1957) and corrected in Chapter 8. My version departs from Chapter 8 in three minor ways: (1) I couch everything in terms of asymmetric relations $(P_i, \succ)$ where Arrow prefers reflexive ones $(R_i, \succcurlyeq)$; because they are interdefinable, the difference is stylistic. (2) I have restricted individual preference orderings to linear ones. (3) I strengthened $\mathbf{D}$ a bit by adding the qualification "when everyone else disagrees." It is not needed for Arrow's Theorem (though it simplifies the proof) because we can infer from his other assumptions that if $\{i\}$ is universally decisive (contrary to my $\mathbf{D}$), then so is every superset of $\{i\}$. But that inference is no longer possible after we relax $\mathbf{T}$ to **Acyclicity** in Chapter 4, and it is simpler to keep **AUD I** intact for all the theorems of this and the next chapter. That will help me reuse the proof of Arrow's Theorem, with very small modifications, for the more important impossibility theorems to come.

But for the record, call i a *dictator* if every g containing i is universally decisive. Suppose $\{i\}$ is universally decisive (as deduced in my proof). To show that i is a dictator, take any $\mathbf{P}$ and any x, y with xP_iy. Construct $\mathbf{P}'$ so that $xP'_izP'_iy$ and $zP'_jxP'_jy$ for every $j \neq i$ with xP_jy, and zP_kyP_kx for every other k. Then $x \succ_{\mathbf{p}'} z$ because $\{i\}$ is universally decisive, and $z \succ_{\mathbf{p}'} y$ by $\mathbf{U}$, so $x \succ_{\mathbf{p}'} y$ by $\mathbf{T}$, whence $x \succ_{\mathbf{p}'} y$ by $\mathbf{I}$.

Arrow's mistake about **I** is from p. 27 of his 1963 book. Plott (1976) exposed it. Especially in the spoiler version, the mistake is often repeated, as is the confusion between the Borda Rule and that unimplementable variant.

CHAPTER 4

Sen (1970a, Chapters 7, 7*) proclaimed the virtue of social partial orderings, of relaxing **T** to ≻–**Transitivity**. The theorem which challenges that by adding **MR** to **AUDI** is new. Instead of **MR**, an older, less simple result strengthens **D** to a ban on *oligarchies*. They are universally decisive sets whose members have universal *blocking* power: by preferring x to y, each member can prevent $y \succ x$, or ensure $x \succcurlyeq y$ (but maybe not $x \succ y$). The editor made me delete a long footnote about that from my 1970 article. Sen (1970a, p. 49) mentions the result with attribution to a class paper by Alan Gibbard. The first published proof is in Mas Colell and Sonnenschein (1972). It is simpler just to ban universal blockers (as in my 1986 book, p. 59) and simpler still to keep **AUDI** intact and add **MR**. Here and elsewhere, as promised at the outset, I have tried to keep a long story short by omitting needless complexity, inconsequential variation, and scholarly qualification.

The cycle theorem based on **A+** and **MR** is a special case of my 1970 result, the first Arrovian impossibility theorem based on **Acyclicty** (which I then called Noncircularity). I present an improved version of that theorem in Section 4.6. Like the original of 1970, it allows interpersonal utility comparisons and, therefore, relaxes **I** to a faint palimpsest of itself. Add back the full force of **I** (which implies ordinality) and you obviously have the result of Section 4.2, based on **A+** and **MR**, my reason for attributing that result to the 1970 paper.

The meretricious Positive Responsiveness is from Mas Collel and Sonnenschein (1972), the "$n/5$" variant from my 1982b article, the "$n/3$" variant of Duggan from a private communication, and the refutation of all such assumptions from my 2001 article.

The cycle theorem based on $(2k - 2)\mathbf{R}$ is also from that article.

CHAPTER 5

The cited theorems are those of Ward (1960), Sen (1970a, pp. 78–88), Brown (1975), and Nakamura (1979). The two results about **IP** (sufficiency and necessity) are from my 2007 article. The decisive-set equivalents of (*) and **IP** are similar to the condition of Ferejohn and Fishburn (1979), but the latter assume that the pairs (x_i, y_i) are cyclically linked: $y_1 = x_2, y_2 = x_3, \ldots, y_m = x_1$. To drop that restriction, I paid the small price of assuming **U** or **U+**.

CHAPTER 6

This is all new.

CHAPTER 7

The idea that cycles and other intransitivities ensure manipulability is new. The other manipulability theorems are from Gibbard (1973), Satterthwaite (1975), and Duggan and Schwartz (2000). Taylor's 2002 article offers a more readable exposition, his 2002 book a treatise on the subject of manipulation. To this day, ignorant scholars cite Gibbard–Satterthwaite as showing what it does not show.

It was Wilson (1972) who first saw the connection between social choice and cooperative game theory. Maskin (1999) proved the necessity of **MM** for Nash-implementation. I found the incompatibility of **MM** with cycles through joint work with John Duggan.

CHAPTER 8

The idea of strategic voting on agendas goes back to Farquharson (1969), the correct definitions to McKelvey and Niemi (1978) and Moulin (1979). On the control of agenda trees, see Ordeshook and Schwartz (1987) and Schwartz (2008). The former treats of generic agendas; the latter adds Anglo-American and Euro-Latin along with the hybrid Mex-Italian variety. Earlier theorems and proofs about the extent of agenda power were all wrong, as shown by Ordeshook and Schwartz, owing to a faulty definition of agenda trees: *most* real agendas fail to fit that definition (including ones expressly offered as illustrations of the definition). Hammond (1986) has shown that tree control is tantamount to the control of bureaucratic structure. Chernoff (1954) stated his condition.

On essential packages, see Chapter 2 citations. Essential anti-packages and the two general cycle results are new.

The veto paradox is from my 1999 article, the version with simple-majority override from my 2004 article. Constructive forms of veto power, not only the item veto but the various types of strong amendatory veto found in Latin America, also have paradoxical consequences, as shown by Aleman and myself (2006). The paradox of representation comes from my 1994 article. Related monotonicity paradoxes show that a candidate can profit from a drop in rank on preferential ballots (Hoag and Hallet 1926, p. 398), a chairman from a loss of tie-breaking power (Farquharson 1969, pp. 50 f.), a voter from not showing up (Brams and Fishburn 1983).

The idea of majority-rule externalities leading to Pareto-inefficiencies is from Buchanan and Tullock (1962). The idea of parties as long coalitions is from my unpublished (but widely cited) paper, "Why Parties?" developed further (and better) by Aldrich's book of the same name. The connection to cycles is new – and is the missing piece that kept me from finishing my old paper for publication. Among the countless writings about parties that begin by assuming away the reason parties exist, the most famous is Downs (1957).

CHAPTER 9

Defined and axiomatically characterized in my 1990 article, *TEQ* has been examined by Brandt, Brill, Fischer, and Harrenstein (2010), by Brandt, Chudnovksy, Kim, Norin, Scott, Seymour, Thommasé, and Montpelier (2011), by Brandt, Fischer, and Harrenstein (2009), by Brandt, Fischer, Harrenstein, and Mair (2010), by Lafford, Laslier, and Le Breton (1993) by Laslier (1997), by Houy (2009), and by Moser (2012). The comparative study of tournament solutions is mostly rooted in the seminal and very readable essay of Moulin (1986).

When ties are allowed, there are two versions of the top-cycle set. They are the GETCHA and GOCHA sets of my 1986 book, Section 6.1. The GOCHA set is from my 1970 and 1972 articles, the GETCHA set from my 1977 article. The latter is equivalent to a solution set of Ferejohn and Grether (1974). GOCHA and GETCHA are equivalent when ties are absent, but in general the GETCHA set is more inclusive. Applied to α, it is the $\subseteq$ – least subset β of α with $x \succ y$ for all $x \in \beta$, $y \in \alpha - \beta$, and the GOCHA set is the union of $\subseteq$ – least subsets β of α with $x \succ y$ for no $x \in \alpha - \beta$, $y \in \beta$. Deb (1977) showed that any form of top cycle based on majority preferences can have Pareto-inefficient members.

The uncovered set was defined by Miller (1980) and Fishburn (1977), the Banks set by Banks (1985), the minimum covering set by Dutta (1988). The subset relationships are from my 1990 article and then Dutta (1990). The uncovered and Banks sets were originally proposed as solutions for strategic voting on agenda trees, but that was based on an erroneous definition of agenda trees, corrected by Ordeshook and Schwartz (1987).

SC is the condition that turns $TC(\alpha)$ into the SOCO set of my 1986 book, Chapter 7. The "neighborhood" generalization of TEQ comes from Moser (2012).

"Why So Much Stability?" is Tullock's (1981) famous title. Structure-induced equilibrium is widely discussed. The chief sources are Shepsle (1979) and Shepsle and Weingast (1981).

CHAPTER 10

Young (1974) and Saari (2006) offer defenses of the Borda Rule, Brams and Fishburn (1978) the invention and extensive study of the Approval Rule. The famous (but weak) argument that Plurality Rule encourages a two-party system is Duverger's (1959).

I discuss grading as a social-choice mechanism in my 2011 article. Smith (2000) introduced the "average" version, which he called *range voting*, Balinski and Laraki (2010) the "median" version, which they called *the majority judgment*.

My critique of preference-based welfare judgments is based on a 1982a essay.

The suggested restriction on individual preference orderings is a relaxation of Blau's (1957) "free triple" restriction.

It was Packard (1975c) who saw how a slight relaxation of individual transitivity makes it trivial to derive a $\succ$–cycle.

Besides my 1970 and (esp.) 1972 articles and my 1986 book, the reinterpretation of cyclic social preferences as cyclic *individual* preferences, contrary to individual "rationality," is suggested by May (1954), Tversky (1969), Packard (1975a, b, and 1982), and Arrow and Raynaud (1986).

The characterization theorem based on (1)–(3) is new. But in my 2015 article I took a similar approach to game solutions: even unique and strict Nash equilibria are often dumb things to predict, but not when we generalize the conventional definition so that strategies can *vary in specificity.*

References

Aldrich, John H. 1995. *Why Parties?* Chicago: University of Chicago Press.

Aleman, Eduardo, and Thomas Schwartz. 2006. "Presidential Vetoes in Latin American Constitutions." *Journal of Theoretical Politics* 18: 98–120.

Arrow, Kenneth J. 1950. "A Difficulty in the Concept of Social Welfare." *Journal of Political Economy* 58: 328–346

Arrow, Kenneth J. 1952. *Social Choice and Individual Values.* 1st edn. New York: Wiley

Arrow, Kenneth J. 1959. "Rational Choice Functions and Orderings." *Economica* [N.S.] 26: 121–127.

Arrow, Kenneth J. 1963. *Social Choice and Individual Values.* 2nd edn. New Haven, CT: Yale University Press. First edition published by Wiley, 1951.

Arrow, Kenneth J. and Hervé Reynaud. 1986. *Social Choice and Multicriterion Decision-Making.* Cambridge, MA: MIT Press.

Balinski, Michel, and Rida Laraki. 2010. *Majority Judgment.* Cambridge, MA: MIT Press.

Banks, Jeffrey S. 1985. "Sophisticated Voting Outcomes and Agenda Control." *Social Choice and Welfare* 2: 295–306.

Bernholz, Peter. 1973. "Logrolling, Arrow Paradox and Cyclical Majorities." *Public Choice* 15: 87–95.

Bernholz, Peter. 1974. "Logrolling, Arrow Paradox and Decision Rules – A Generalization." *Kyklos* 27: 49–61.

Black, Duncan. 1948. "On the Rationale of Group Decision-Making." *Journal of Political Economy* 56: 23–24.

Black, Duncan. 1958. *Theory of Committees and Elections.* Cambridge: Cambridge University Press.

Black, Duncan and R. A. Newing. 1951. *Committee Decisions with Complementary Valuation.* London: William Hodge.

Blau, Julian H. 1957. "The Existence of Social Welfare Functions." *Econometrica* 25: 302–313.

Borda, Jean-Charles. 1781. "Memoires sur les Électroniques au Scrutin." *Histoires de l'Academie Royale des Sciences.* English translation by A. de Grazia. "Mathematical Derivation of an Election System." *Iris* 44 (1953).

Brams, Steven and Peter Fishburn. 1983. "Paradoxes of Preferential Voting." *Mathematical Magazine* 56: 207–214.

Brandt, F., F. Fischer, and P. Harrenstein. 2009. "A Computational Analysis of the Tournament Equilibrium Set." *Social Choice and Welfare* 34: 597–609.

Brandt, F., F. Fischer, and P. Harrenstein. 2009. "The Computational Complexity of Choice Sets." *Mathematical Logic Quarterly* 55: 444–459.

Brandt, F., M. Brill, F. Fischer, and P. Harrenstein. 2014. "Minimal Retentive Sets in Tournaments." *Social Choice and Welfare* 42: 551–574.

Brandt, F., M. Chudnovsky, I. Kim, S. Norin, A. Scott, P. Seymour, S. Thomassé, and F. Montpelier. 2011. "A Counterexample to a Conjecture of Schwartz." *Social Choice and Welfare* 40: 739–743.

Brown, Donald J. 1975. "Aggregation of Preferences." *Quarterly Journal of Economics* 89: 456–469.

Buchanan, James M. and Gordon Tullock. 1962. *The Calculus of Consent*. Ann Arbor, MI: University of Michigan Press.

Chernoff, Herman. 1954. "Rational Selection of Decision Functions." *Econometrica* 22: 422–443.

Condorcet, the Marquis de. 1785. *Essai sur l'application de l'analyse à la probabilité des decisions rendues à la pluralité des voix*. Paris. Trans. as "Essay on the Application of Mathematics to the theory of Decision Making." In K. Baker, ed., *Condorcet, Selected Writings*. Indianapolis: Bobbs-Merrill, 1976.

Cox, Gary. 1987. "The Uncovered Set and the Core." *American Journal of Political Science* 31: 408–422.

Davis, Otto A. and Melvin J. Hinich. 1966. "A Mathematical Model of Policy Formation in a Democratic Society." In Joseph Bernd, ed., *Mathematical Applications in Political Science*, Vol. II. Dallas, TX: Southern Methodist University Press, pp. 175–208.

Deb, Rajat. 1977. "On Schwartz's Rule." *Journal of Economic Theory* 16: 103–110.

Downs, Anthony. 1957. *An Economic Theory of Democracy*. New York: Harper & Row.

Duggan, John and Thomas Schwartz. 2000. "Strategic Manipulation without Resoluteness or Shared Beliefs: Gibbard-Satterthwaite Generalized." *Social Choice and Welfare* 17: 85–93.

Dutta, Baskar. 1988. "Covering Sets and a New Condorcet Choice Correspondence." *Journal of Economic Theory* 44: 63–68.

Dutta, Baskar. 1990. "On the Tournament Equilibrium Set." *Social Choice and Welfare* 7: 381–383.

Duverger, Maurice. 1959. "Political Parties." *Political Science* 31: 408–422.

Enelow, James M. and Melvin Hinich. 1984. *An Introduction to the Spatial Theory of Voting*. Cambridge: Cambridge University Press.

Farquharson, Robin. 1969. *Theory of Voting*. New Haven, CT: Yale University Press.

Ferejohn, John. 1985. "Logrolling in an Institutional Context: A Case Study of Food Stamps Legislation." Unpublished MS. Stanford University, California.

Ferejohn, John A. and David Grether. 1974. "On a Class of Rational Social Decision Procedures." *Journal of Economic Theory* 8: 471–482.

Ferejohn, John A. and Peter C. Fishburn. 1979. "Representation of Binary Decision Rules by Generalized Decision Structures." *Journal of Economic Theory* 21: 28–45.

Fishburn, Peter C. 1973. *The Theory of Social Choice*. Princeton, NJ: Princeton University Press.

Fishburn, Peter C. 1977. "Condorcet Social Choice Functions." *Siam Journal of Applied Mathematics* 33: 469–489.

Fishburn, Peter C. and Steven J. Brams. 1978. "Approval Voting." *American Political Science Review* 72: 831–847.

Gehrlein, William V. 1983. "Condorcet's Paradox." *Theory and Decision* 15: 161–197.

Gibbard, Allan. 1973. "Manipulation of Voting Schemes: *A General Result*." *Econometrica* 41: 587–601.

Hammond, Thomas. 1986. "Agenda Control, Organizational Structure, and Bureaucratic Politics." *American Journal of Political Science* 30: 379–420.

Hammond, Thomas, and Gary. Miller 1987. "The Core of the Constitution." *American Political Science Review* 81: 1155–1175.

Hoag, Clarence, G. and George H. Hallet, Jr. 1926. *Proportional Representation*. New York: Macmillan.

Hotelling, Harold. 1929. "Stability in Competition." *The Economic Journal* 39: 41–57. Reprinted in George J. Stigler and Kenneth E. Boulding, eds., *Readings in Price Theory*, Chicago, IL: Irwin, 1952, pp. 467–485.

Houy, N. 2009. "Still More on the Tournament Equilibrium Set." *Social Choice and Welfare* 32: 93–99.

Inada, K.-I. 1969. "On the Simple Majority Decision Rule." *Econometrica* 37: 490–506.

International Conference on Autonomous Agents and Multiagent Systems (AAMAS 2010). Toronto.

Kadane, J. B. 1972. "On Division of the Question." *Public Choice* 13: 47–54.

Koford, Kenneth. 1989. "Dimensions in Congressional Voting." *American Political Science Review* 83: 949–962.

Krehbiel, Keith. 1998. *Pivotal Politics: A Theory of U.S. Lawmaking*: Chicago, IL: University of Chicago Press.

Lafford, G., J-F. Laslier, and M. Le Breton. 1993. "More on the Tournament Equilibrium Set." *Mathématiques et Science Humaines* 31: 37–44.

Lasslier, J.-F. 1997. *Soultions and Majority Voting*. Berlin: Springer.

Mas-Colell, Andreu and Hugo F. Sonnenschein. 1972. "General Possibility Theorems for Group Decisions." *Review of Economic Studies* 39: 185–192.

Maskin, Eric. 1999. "Nash Equilibrium and Welfare Optimality." *Review of Economic Studies* 66: 23–38.

May, K. O. 1954. "Intransitivity, Utility and the Aggregation of Preference Patterns." *Econometrica* 22: 1–13.

McGarvey, D. C. 1953. "A Theorem on the Construction of Voting Paradoxes." *Econometrica* 21: 608–610.

McKelvey, Richard D. 1976. "Intransitivities in Multidimensional Voting Models, and Some Implications for Agenda Control." *Journal of Economic Theory* 2: 472–482.

McKelvey, Richard D. and Norman Schofield. 1987. "Generalized Symmetry Conditions at a Core Point." *Econometrica* 55: 923–933.

McKelvey, Richard D. and Richard Niemi. 1978. "A Multi-Stage Game Representation of Sophisticated Voting for Binary Procedures." *Journal of Economic Theory* 18: 1–22.

McLean, Iain and Arnold B. Urken. 1995. *Classics of Social Choice*. Ann Arbor, MI: University of Michigan Press.

Miller, Nicholas. 1980. "A New Solution Set for Tournaments and Majority Voting: Further Graph Theoretical Approaches to the Theory of Voting." *American Journal of Political Science* 24: 68–96.

Moser, Scott. 2012. "A Note on Contestation-Based Tournament Solutions." *Social Choice and Welfare* 41: 133–143.

Moser, Scott and Daniel Allock. 2013. "Binary Relations from Tournament Solutions, and Back Again." Unpublished MS, University of Texas+.

Moulin, Hervé. 1979. "Dominance-Solvable Voting Schemes." *Econometrica* 47: 1134–1151.

Moulin, Hervé. 1986. "Choosing from a Tournament." *Social Choice and Welfare* 3: 271–291.

Nakamura, K. 1979. "The Vetoers in a Simple Game with Ordinal Preferences." *International Journal of Game Theory* 8: 55–61.

Nash, John F. 1950. "The Bargaining Problem." *Econometrica* 18: 155–162.

Oppenheimer, Joe A. 1975. "Some Political Implications of 'Vote Trading and the Voting Paradox: A Proof of Logical Equivalence.'" *American Political Science Review* 69: 963–966.

Ordeshook, Peter C. and Thomas Schwartz. 1987. "Agendas and the Control of Political Outcomes." *American Political Science Review* 81: 179–199.

Packard, Dennis J. 1975a. "A Note on Wiitgenstein and Cyclical Comparatives." *Analysis* 36: 37–40.

Packard, Dennis J. 1975b. "On the Impossibility of Measurement." *Utah Academy Proceedings* 52 (2): 36–43.

Packard, Dennis J. 1975c. "Social Choice Theory and Citizens' Intransitive Weak Preference." *Public Choice* 22: 107–111.

Packard, Dennis J. 1982. "Cyclical Preference Logic." *Theory and Decision* 14: 415–426.

Pattanaik, Prasanta K. 1971. *Voting and Collective Choice*. London and New York: Cambridge University Press.

Plott, Charles. 1967. "A Notion of Equilibrium and Its Possibility under Majority Rule." *American Economic Review* 57: 788–806.

Plott, Charles. 1976. "Axiomatic Social Choice Theory: An Overview and Interpretation." *American Journal of Political Science* 20: 511–596.

Poole, Keith and Howard Rosenthal. 1985. "A Spatial Model for Legislative Roll Call Analysis." *American Journal of Political Science* 29: 357–384.

Poole, Keith and Howard Rosenthal. 1997. *Congress*. Oxford: Oxford University Press.

Romer, Thomas and Howard Rosenthal. 1978. "Political Resource Allocation, Controlled Agendas and the Status Quo." *Public Choice* 33: 27–43.

Saari, Donald. 2006. "Which is Better: The Condorcet or Borda Winner?" *Social Choice and Welfare* 26: 107–130.

Satterthwaite, Mark A. 1975. "Strategy-Proofness and Arrow's Conditions: Existence and Correspondence Theorems for Voting Procedures and Social Welfare Functions." *Journal of Economic Theory* 10: 187–217.

Schofield, Norman. 1978. "Instability of Simple Dynamic Games." *Review of Economic Studies* 45: 575–594.

Schwartz, Thomas. 1970. "On the Possibility of Rational Policy Evaluation." *Theory and Decision* 1: 89–106.

Schwartz, Thomas. 1972. "Rationality and the Myth of the Maximum." *Nous* 6: 97–117.

Schwartz, Thomas. 1977. "Collective Choice, Separation of Issues, and Vote Trading." *American Political Science Review* 71: 999–1010.

Schwartz, Thomas. 1981. "The Universal Instability Theorem." *Public Choice* 37: 487–501.

Schwartz, Thomas. 1982a. "Human Welfare: What It Is Not." In Harlan Miller and William Williams, eds., *The Limits of Utilitarianism*, pp. 195–206. Minneapolis, MN: University of Minnesota Press.

Schwartz, Thomas. 1982b. "A Really General Impossibility Theorem." *Quality and Quantity* 16: 493–505.

Schwartz, Thomas. 1986. *The Logic of Collective Choice*. New York: Columbia University Press

Schwartz, Thomas. 1990. "Cyclic Tournaments and Cooperative Majority Voting: A Solution." *Social Choice and Welfare* 7: 19–292.

Schwartz, Thomas. 1994. "The Paradox of Representation." *The Journal of Politics* 57: 309–323.

Schwartz, Thomas. 1999. "The Executive Veto: Purpose, Procedure, and Paradox." *Constitutional Political Economy* 10: 89–105.

Schwartz, Thomas. 2001. "From Arrow to Cycles, Instability, and Chaos by Untying Alternatives." *Social Choice and Welfare* 18: 1–22.

Schwartz, Thomas. 2004. "Vetoes Overridable by Simple Majorities." *Constitutional Political Economy* 15: 383–389.

Schwartz, Thomas. 2007. "A Procedural Condition Necessary and Sufficient for Cyclic Social Preference." *Journal of Economic Theory* 37: 688–695.

Schwartz, Thomas. 2008. "Parliamentary Procedure: Principal Forms and Political Effects." *Public Choice* 36: 353–377.

Schwartz, Thomas. 2011. "One-Dimensionality and Stability in Legislative Voting." *Public Choice* 48: 197–214.

Schwartz, Thomas. 2011. "Social Choice and Individual Values in the Electronic Republic." *Social Choice and Welfare* 37: 621–632.

Schwartz, Thomas. 2015. "Rational Interplay: A Philosophical Critique and Revision of Nash Equilibrium." *Journal of Business and Economics* 20: 680–684.

Sen, Amartya K. 1970a. *Collective Choice and Social Welfare*. San Francisco: Holden-Day.

Sen, Amartya. 1970b. "The Impossibility of a Paretian Liberal." *Journal of Political Economy* 78: 152–157.

Sen, Amartya K. and Prasanta Pattanaik. 1969. "Necessary and Sufficient Conditions for Rational Choice Under Majority Decision." *Journal of Economic Theory* 1: 178–202.

Shepsle, Kenneth A. 1979. "Institutional Arrangements and Equilibrium in Multidimensional Voting Models." *American Journal of Political Science* 23: 27–59.

Shepsle, Kenneth A. and Barry Weingast. 1981. "Structure-Induced Equilibrium and Legislative Choice." *Public Choice* 37: 503–519.

Smith, W. D. 2000. "Range Voting." wds/homepage/rangevote.pdf.

Taylor, Alan D. 2002. "The Manipulability of Voting Systems." *The American Mathematics Monthly* 109: 321–337.

Taylor, Alan D. 2005. *Social Choice and the Mathematics of Manipulation.* Cambridge: Cambridge University Press.

Taylor, Alan D. and Allison M. Pacelli. 2008. *Mathematics and Politics.* New York: Springer.

Tsebelis, George. 2002. *Veto Players: How Political Institutions Work.* Princeton, NJ: Princeton University Press.

Tullock, Gordon. 1981. "Why So Much Stability?" *Public Choice* 37: 189–204.

Tversky, Amos. 1969. "Intransitivity of Preferences." *Psychological Review* 76: 31–48.

Ward, Benjamin. 1960. "Majority Rule and Allocation." *Journal of Conflict Resolution* 5: 380–389.

Wilson, Robert. 1972a. "The Game-Theoretic Structure of Arrow's General Possibility Theorem." *Journal of Economic Theory* 5: 14–20.

Young, H. P. 1974. "An Axiomatization of Borda's Rule." *Journal of Economic Theory* 9: 43–52.

Index